ADVANCE PRAISE

"We are at a moment of collective transition, and one that appears to reflect a hierarchy of human needs and a deepening understanding of the ways in which those unmet needs can manifest as physical illness. As a practicing psychiatrist, I have personally witnessed the increasingly limited yield of the doctor-patient dyad in lieu of community-based healing, and have been forced to recognize what James Maskell has been declaring for years: we heal faster, deeper, and more easefully in the group setting. It's time for us to reweave the fabric of our ancestry and to resolve the isolation of modular living by coming together with a shared intention to take personal responsibility for our health, but to do it together. James is the perfect ambassador for this mission."

—DR. KELLY BROGAN, *NEW YORK TIMES* BESTSELLING
AUTHOR AND HOLISTIC PSYCHIATRIST

"In my research, I have come to understand loneliness and social isolation as a key driver of chronic disease, and this book provides a real solution to address this growing epidemic."

—DALLAS HARTWIG, *NEW YORK TIMES* BESTSELLING AUTHOR, FOUNDER, WHOLE30

"Over the past decade, James Maskell has shown a penchant for focusing the integrative and functional medicine communities on the most important work ahead. He's taken on issues related to necessary efficiencies in care delivery—to keep practice costs down—and the massive influence of behavioral determinants of health. With his series of exceptional interviews and this book on group-delivered services he has hit a trifecta. Groups make the most sense for delivering the mind-and-body integrative interventions for lifestyle change. They are a goldmine for cost saving in an industry that has been wanton in its consumption of resources. And they go straight to resolving the critical access issues that keep less-resourced people from the benefits of integrative care. It helps too, that the evidence on how adults like to learn, change, and transform is in interactive, group environments. This is a book for our time and I earnestly hope every clinician will begin their exploration asking where and in what ways they can work group methods more deeply into their own practices. Maskell brings the wisdom of the best."

—JOHN WEEKS, EDITOR IN CHIEF, THE JOURNAL OF ALTERNATIVE AND COMPLEMENTARY MEDICINE

THE COMMUNITY CURE

THE

COMMUNITY CURE

TRANSFORMING HEALTH OUTCOMES

— TOGETHER —

JAMES MASKELL

LIONCREST
PUBLISHING

THE COMMUNITY CURE
Transforming Health Outcomes Together

ISBN   978-1-5445-0667-8 *Hardcover*
        978-1-5445-0666-1 *Paperback*
        978-1-5445-0665-4 *Ebook*
        978-1-5445-0732-3 *Audiobook*

In memory of

Gabriel Victor Hoffman

1.27.1981–4.22.2019

*"Empathy isn't just feeling other people's pain,
it is seeing each other as capable."*

CONTENTS

INTRODUCTION: THE STATE OF THE EVOLUTION .. 13

1. A CURE FOR LONELINESS 29

2. THE DOUBTS... 49

3. THE MENTORS..73

4. THE CHALLENGES..97

5. THE TRANSFORMATION... 123

6. YOUR ROADMAP FOR GROUP VISITS.................. 149

7. OUR COLLECTIVE FUTURE..................................... 175

   CONCLUSION: THE COMMUNITY CURE.............. 197

   FURTHER RESOURCES 209

   ACKNOWLEDGMENTS 213

   ABOUT THE AUTHOR... 217

THE STATE OF THE EVOLUTION

When I published my first book in 2016, I had high hopes that empowering physicians to get to the root cause of illness would help eradicate chronic disease. To do this, we needed a different operating system of medicine: one that predicts future disease, prevents issues before they arise, personalizes treatment to the individual, and empowers participation from patients. I argued that this aspiration of "P4 Medicine"—personalized, predictive, preventive, and participatory—is best activated today as functional medicine.

An October 2019 study in the *Journal of the American Medical Association* showed how "functional medicine patients exhibited significantly larger improvements" in outcomes "than were seen in patients treated at a family health center." If only we could inspire enough physicians to understand this emergent way of treating lifestyle-driven disease, make it easy to evolve their practices and support patients affordably, and help them fall back in love with practicing medicine, the rest would take care of itself.

The number of physicians who have made the switch to functional medicine continues to grow quickly, technology to support these practices has improved, and more and more institutions are jumping on the bandwagon. This paradigm shift isn't just limited to the medical system, as communities, organizations, employers, and even sovereign nations realize the current paradigm of care isn't working and see the need for a radical transformation—one that moves away from disease management and toward its reversal, through health creation.

So, in some ways, *The Evolution of Medicine: Join the Movement to Solve Chronic Disease and Fall Back in Love with Medicine* has been a success. Since its publication, I've spoken to thousands of health professionals—at conferences, events, and on our 2018 tour, many of whom have made the switch and seen tremendous value from it, both in their practices and in their personal lives. Yet, like you, I'm still waiting impatiently for the large-scale transformation we all hope for.

In fact, it's really easy to argue it's getting worse.

Instead of lowering rates of chronic disease and increasing life expectancy, we're witnessing an accelerating decline in the health of the population, with life expectancy falling year over year for the first time in recorded history. Physician suicides and malaise continue to grow and the people that truly need access to care aren't getting it.

Exhibit 1: BCBS Health Index by Age (2017)

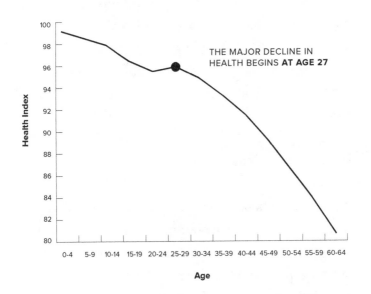

Recently, Blue Cross Blue Shield released a report outlining how Millennials now have higher rates of health conditions than their predecessors at the same age, with their health peaking at age twenty-seven before declining. Not only is this unacceptable from a societal standpoint, it will also prove to be incredibly costly on the health-care system, which is already overly burdened with baby boomers and chronically ill Gen Xers.

The fundamental processes that lead to changes in life expectancy and chronic illness have either not shifted or haven't shifted quickly enough. Yes, the food system is slowly improving (albeit with growing racial disparities), more people have access to stress-reduction strategies like meditation and yoga, more and more people are waking up to the link between lifestyle and disease, and, dare I say it, being healthy is actually becoming cool. These are all lead indicators of future change. But the most significant determinant of disease continues to spread.

We have an epidemic of loneliness.

The smartest people in healthcare are recognizing the impact that the loss of community has on our society, economy, and health. Over the last few years there has been a glut of books, articles, and exposés showing the incredible impact of social isolation on our mental and physical health.

A 2018 survey completed by Cigna, showed that half of Americans feel alone, isolated or left out at least some of the time, with Millennials and Gen-Z being the loneliest generations ever. Douglas Nemecek, MD, the Chief Medical Officer of Cigna, is quoted as saying that being lonely, "has the same impact on mortality as smoking fifteen cigarettes a day, making it even more dangerous than obesity."

How did this happen?

In his book *The Third Pillar: How Markets and the State Leave the Community Behind*, Raghuram Rajan chronicles our collective history right back to the Dark Ages, and how technology—accelerated through the industrial revolution and subsequently the information technology revolution—have ripped apart the fabric of traditional communities. Formerly the chief economist of the International Monetary Fund, the author shows that although we are more interconnected in certain ways, we are largely much more isolated than ever before.

For thousands of years, multiple generations lived under the same roof or within the same town. It really wasn't all that long ago that people sourced everything they needed from where they lived, trading and bartering for goods and services with locals. People knew their neighborhood grocer or had personal relationships with shopkeepers and tradespeople. Communities were interdependent—relying on one another for survival.

Now, the majority of goods we purchase or consume are sourced from individuals we don't know. The invention of the automobile allowed people to move into the suburbs and live in isolated single family homes. Bustling downtown streets went quiet, and brick-and-mortar businesses in city centers were superseded by shopping centers and strip malls. Within just a few decades, all of this was replaced by the internet, which allows us to source anything we could ever imagine online, without ever having to step foot outside our homes. While this has many advantages, it has dramatically altered the context and experience of togetherness.

Charles Eisenstein's seminal work *Sacred Economics* describes how we've shifted from the gift economy into an age of separation, one in which we are "helplessly independent." We're self-sufficient to the people we know, but totally dependent on strangers living miles, if not oceans, away.

With families and communities no longer meeting the majority of our needs, it has led to total commodification—meaning we need ever more money to pay for our babysitters, grief counselors and elder care, once a burden shared by the community itself.

As a result we are constantly looking to the economy, the market, the state, or the government to solve our problems. The death of community has led to a myopic view of the world, in which the market and government are our only two options for solutions.

This is especially poignant when it comes to healthcare. 2020 is a watershed moment for the United States, as the Republicans and Democrats elected this year could change the trajectory of how we solve this problem. Will it be the markets or government that will solve for the healthcare we need?

This outlook ignores what Rajan calls *The Third Pillar:* community.

What if we stopped waiting for other people to solve the problem, and build the solution around this third pillar?

In my first book, I gave the example of the Blue Zones: five regions of the world where the population lives longer with little evidence of chronic disease, independent of access to sophisticated medical systems. In Sardinia, Okinawa, the Nicoya Peninsula of Costa Rica, Icaria, and the Seventh Day Adventists in Loma Linda, California, these populations eat well, engage in physical activity, and lead lives with low stress. But one of the key components of Blue Zones are strong communities. Not only is having a supportive community healthy in itself, but the culture reinforces the ongoing healthy behaviors that lead to long-term health. Their resilient networks are what drive their health outcomes—not medical systems.

We've known for a long time that Blue Zones aren't a fluke. They're a perfect example of a biopsychosocial model, where social factors like relationships, peers, and socioeconomic status play an equal role to biological and psychological factors.

A 1988 study published in *Science* by House, Landis, and Umberson showed how mortality risk decreases as social integration increases, across multiple countries and cultures. Furthermore, a 2010 study in *PLoS Medicine* concluded "the influence of social relationships on risk for mortality is comparable with well-established risk factors for mortality." Not just comparable; in most cases, social isolation is a bigger determinant on health and disease than any other factor.

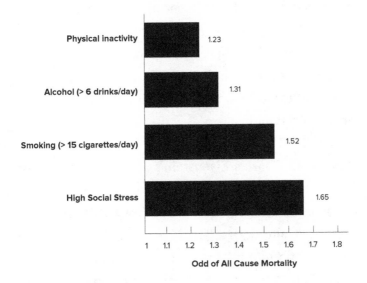

Risk for Chronic Disease-Related Mortality

Physical Inactivity — 1.23
Alcohol (> 6 drinks/day) — 1.31
Smoking (> 15 cigarettes/day) — 1.52
High Social Stress — 1.65

Odd of All Cause Mortality

With ever-improving technology, we're learning more about the mechanism: what's actually happening. George Slavich, PhD of UCLA Laboratory for Stress Assessment and Research, has taken our understanding of this to the cellular level with the emerging science of Human Social Genomics. For instance, if you are subject to a targeted rejection—a very clear intention to break a social bond, such as in a divorce or getting fired from your job—your risk of depression is more than twenty times higher than with other types of life stress.

Loneliness has an unequivocal impact on our health.

People who are lonely have more difficulty recovering

from acute illness and struggle more with chronic disease. Socially isolated individuals end up in the medical system not just because they are more likely to be sick, but also because they don't have anyone to talk to. Even when patients get better, physicians report patients return just to be able to talk to someone. I've witnessed this firsthand in my own family.

Similar to Charles Eisenstein's sentiments in *Sacred Economics*, "Long ago I grew tired of reading books that criticized some aspect of our society without offering a positive alternative. Then I grew tired of books that offered a positive alternative that seemed impossible to reach [...]. Then I grew tired of books that offered a plausible method of reaching it, but did not describe what I could personally do to create it."

This is why *The Community Cure* exists. I have been fortunate in the last decade to bear witness to a solution so simple and elegant that, once you understand it, you can't un-think it.

It isn't costly, we don't need more clinical trials, and it doesn't have a decade-long runway to bring it to market. By the end of this book you will have everything you need to enact this solution for yourself, whether you are directly involved in the delivery of healthcare, or someone looking to rediscover or maintain good health.

The answer is transforming health outcomes together, in groups.

This is not a new concept, but when existing group models are paired with a functional medicine approach, there's an incredible recipe for true, lasting transformation.

Sometimes referred to as shared medical appointments, group visits bring people together to sit in circles and connect as humans in exactly the same ways we have for millennia. With this simple approach, not only can we solve social isolation, we also create structures that allow for accountability, and consistent application of the fundamentals of health creation.

Reestablishing community through group visits can dynamically solve the social determinants of health for some of the poorest and most vulnerable members of our society. Some groups started more than twenty years ago and still meet weekly to this day. I have seen individuals transform, leaving behind shame, guilt and pain, and finding trust, companionship, and self-efficacy.

And what's more, the heroes of this story, the pioneers leading the movement are not necessarily just doctors. A midwife dramatically improved the dismal rates of infant mortality, and a hospital administrator created new ways of reversing chronic illness inside a storied medical institution, and a group of uninsured immigrants inspired a physician to create the first empowerment groups.

Since I moved to America from England fifteen years ago, I've been passionately committed to solving one of the world's most vexing problems: the cost of chronic illness. My education in health economics alerted me to the size and scope of the problem facing all countries, regardless of development level. The problem is also personal for me. My mother lives in England, my father lives in South Africa, and I've witnessed the same problems in countries across the globe: the cost of treating chronic illness with a pharmaceutical-first approach is bankrupting every medical system, no matter who is paying the bill.

In 2005, my first opportunity at a clinic afforded me first-hand insight into the transformative potential of a new way of delivering medicine to reverse chronic illness. There, diagnoses from Type 2 diabetes to lupus were reversed under the care of the empathetic practitioner. The more I looked, the more I saw this occurring in clinics across the country. It became my life's work to ensure this caliber of care is accessible for everyone.

In 2014, we created the Functional Forum: a community in New York for doctors, health practitioners, and digital entrepreneurs interested in functional medicine. Bringing together physicians who were previously isolated in their practices, establishing a network that resulted in practitioners on six continents feeling more confident delivering a new standard of care within their communities. It became the world's largest functional medical conference, with an episode every month for over six years, hundreds of podcasts, two online summits, and a multi-city tour.

In 2016, we realized that knowing about functional medicine wasn't enough to help physicians actualize it day to day, so we created the Practice Accelerator as a peer-to-peer community to support doctors on that journey in transforming their practices.

In 2018, we created Knew Health, a medical cost sharing community. This is the first non-denominational medical cost sharing community and an affordable alternative to health insurance for Americans, growing access to functional medicine.

Though the majority of my work has been conducted within the United States, I'm here for worldwide transformation. The purpose of this book is to unleash that potential.

Whether you're a physician, a health professional, administrator, CEO or anyone who feels the impacts that lack of community has on the lives of those around you, this book is your guide to change. By launching and scaling group visits, we can solve issues of access, affordability, health creation, and social isolation.

In chapter one, we're going to showcase the pioneers addressing chronic disease by treating loneliness. Chapter two addresses the common doubts that arise when health professionals think about organizing and running group visits. In chapter three, you'll meet the mentors who blazed the trail and built the foundation for this movement. Chapter four tackles the challenges that arise when executing groups and how to surmount them. In chapter five, we'll discover how this model is transforming patient health across the globe, from Puerto Rico to Kosovo, and is equally transformative for practitioners and their clinics. Chapter six will give you the tools to advocate for, organize and run group visits, including further resources. We'll look toward the future of medicine in chapter seven, and see where innovation will likely take this movement. The conclusion provides a unifying thesis for maximizing healthspan with the minimum possible costs, with a model that's relevant for every country and every payer in healthcare.

The most exciting aspect of group visits is that it's not bound to the limitations of the medical systems. Throughout the book, we'll look at leaders and innovators who are thinking outside the system to create lasting and possibly even *exponential* change.

We want to empower you to participate in this movement, building and supporting the reemergence of community at every level of society, starting with healthcare—where isolated individuals end up, and where there's already a budget allocated to solve the problem.

I'm not saying it's going to be easy, but it is totally necessary. My last book provided only an incremental plan to transform health—necessary but not sufficient to solve the problem. The solution in this book has the potential to transform health outcomes rapidly and efficiently, which is critical when facing a problem of this magnitude. With this model, people have radically shifted their own health in as little as ten weeks, and even felt called to support others in the same journey. That impressive turnaround from student to teacher is the backbone of an exponential movement.

But it all starts with you—with us.

As Margaret Mead said, "Never doubt that a small group of thoughtful, committed citizens can change the world. Indeed, it is the only thing that ever has."

CHAPTER ONE

A CURE FOR LONELINESS

"When so many are lonely as seem to be lonely, it would be inexcusably selfish to be lonely alone"

—TENNESSEE WILLIAMS

As a first year resident in 1996, Dr. Jeffrey Geller began to feel like there had to be more to health than just the nuts and bolts of diagnostics and drug-based treatments. His medical career started like most others: with a deep-seated passion for helping people. As a resident, he noticed that patients received the same standard of care, but their outcomes varied significantly. Some patients would arrive with a stubbed toe, for instance, and feel as though they were completely disabled, with their world crashing down around them. Other patients with the same stubbed toe would continue on with their days happily and healthily, as if it were a minor disruption or inconvenience.

Dr. Geller started to wonder why some people portrayed resilience in the face of a medical issue while others completely fell apart.

With each interaction, it became more obvious that the difference between the two groups stemmed from their support systems. People who had support felt engaged and didn't suffer as much with their illness. Those who didn't have support felt alone in their struggle.

Loneliness and lack of social support were some of the main determining factors of the variants in the health outcomes he witnessed.

Dr. Geller conducted award-winning research to back up his observations: people who are lonely visit health centers four to six times more often than those who are not, and visit emergency rooms two to three times more.

According to a study from the AARP Public Policy Institute and Stanford University's Center on the Demography and Economics of Health and Aging, people who were lonely were more likely to have extended hospital stays, more expensive treatments, and need the support of skilled nursing facilities in lieu of support systems to aid in at-home rehabilitation. The participants in the study who were socially isolated had a 50 percent higher risk of death: 35.3 percent of isolated individuals died within six years of the initial interview, whereas 24 percent of those who were connected and 22.3 percent of those who were well connected. Overall, the study found that socially isolated individuals had a 31 percent higher risk of death than those who were not socially isolated.

It's not just mortality, loneliness and isolation is linked to lowered immunity and increased risks for common killers—specifically a 29 percent higher risk for heart disease, 32 percent for stroke, 25 percent for cancer, and 40 percent for Alzheimer's. Another paper on "Loneliness and Social Isolation as Risk Factors for Mortality" found a 26 percent increased likelihood of premature mortality.

The data is unfortunately not surprising, nor is it unknown by practitioners. When Dr. Geller shared his observations from the late 90s, and even when I talk about it now, practitioners are generally in agreement: loneliness is bad for you and significantly impacts health outcomes.

Yet the usual follow-up response is that loneliness doesn't have a billing code. Yes, we acknowledge it's a problem, but if we can't bill for it we can't treat it within the current system. This is true for psychologists, mental health professionals, and medical professionals alike. All parties are on board, but haven't determined a fiscally—and logistically—sound solution to the epidemic of loneliness.

As is typical for a first-year intern, Dr. Geller was swamped with work and severely lacking in sleep. Though he didn't have a lot of free time on his hands, one of his patients, Eduvijes, convinced him to meet her at the library, where she and a group of friends met to discuss their health issues. They were mostly uninsured and intentionally formed this group to support one another. They called it *Si Tú Puedes*, which is Spanish for "yes, you can."

Dr. Geller taught the group about health, and they in turn taught him a bit of Spanish. After some time, he said, "it became clear to me that the relationship with people was so much more important than the actual information I was giving them." The format of *Si Tú Puedes* became the model for the initial group visits.

The first group Dr. Geller started in 1997 and 1998 was ostensibly formed to treat diabetes. He really wanted to cure loneliness, but he knew that wasn't something he could advertise. "If I were to say, 'I'm starting a group for loneliness,' people wouldn't come." Knowing a group founded on loneliness isn't most people's idea of a good time, he needed to find another way to get people in the room. It had to be based on a health issue that they wanted to improve and wouldn't be ashamed to discuss in a group setting.

He secured funding through the CDC and approval from an institutional review board at the University of Massachusetts, which would allow him to research how group visits impacted the health outcomes of patients with diabetes. He didn't bill for the visits. Quickly, and not surprisingly, he witnessed how loneliness was quickly cured when people gathered together. But what about diabetes or other chronic diseases?

For three years, the group met regularly, surmounting a few challenges along the way. Located in an economically disadvantaged community, most of the patients were immigrants who struggled not only with communication barriers, using English as a second language, but with all the other determinants of health. In one of the first meetings, Dr. Geller talked about how eating rice is bad for diabetes. As you can probably imagine, this did not go over well with the group of mostly Hispanic individuals.

Dr. Geller admits, "I didn't quite have the right curriculum off the bat," but people kept coming because they liked each other and the group dynamic.

After three years, participants enjoyed it so much they

asked to bring their families. They felt empowered, and went from being participants to being leaders.

Since the guidelines of the CDC study couldn't accommodate it, Dr. Geller allowed them to organize a second meeting to take place in the same space. They didn't have a budget for Tai Chi lessons or cooking classes, so Dr. Geller asked what they wanted to do with that time. The participants said salsa dancing. "I can't teach you that," Dr. Geller said. "That's okay," the group told him, "we can teach you."

And their health outcomes? "People's loneliness improved, people's depression improved, they lost weight. [...] Blood pressure reduced by 5–10 points, and hemoglobin A1C also reduced, which is a measure of blood sugar and diabetes."

Dr. Geller was able to take the idea that treating loneliness positively impacts health outcomes and turn it into actual medical care that could produce better results than most medications on the market.

What Goes Into Your Health

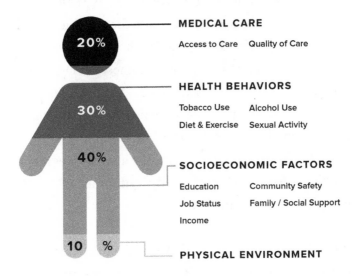

MEDICAL CARE

Access to Care   Quality of Care

HEALTH BEHAVIORS

Tobacco Use   Alcohol Use

Diet & Exercise   Sexual Activity

SOCIOECONOMIC FACTORS

Education   Community Safety

Job Status   Family / Social Support

Income

PHYSICAL ENVIRONMENT

Since the 1990s, Dr. Geller and his team built up to about thirty different types of group visits. At its height, over fifty visits were available weekly at his health center. Some of the initial groups have met weekly for over two decades, continuing to this day. They expanded the groups to work with any illness or issue you could think of: heart disease, prenatal care, hypertension, depression, obesity, addiction, cigarettes, narcotics addiction, and more.

Dr. Geller isn't any different from any other doctor in America, and the community in which he worked is like many across the globe. He was in a poverty-stricken, disadvantaged region, where participants didn't have inordinate access to resources or time. The *Si Tú Puedes* group planted the seed for the cure for loneliness, and for years the participants tended to the crop, resulting in some transformational health outcomes. For Dr. Geller, this group lit the spark for what would become his life's work. He's since started a new practice that runs primarily on group medicine, teaching his Empowerment methodology to physicians, as well as at the annual Integrative Medicine for the Underserved Conference (IM4US), where he serves on the board.

What Dr. Geller essentially discovered more than twenty years ago is a model that is becoming more and more evident as we truly start to understand the web of factors that drive chronic illness.

But what about medical conditions we don't typically categorize as chronic illness?

PREGNANCY AND INFANT MORTALITY

When we think of pregnancy, infant mortality, and preterm birth, it's not seen as an illness per se. But unlike loneliness, it does have a billing code. As such, it's treated as a medical condition within the American health system. And if you're not familiar with the statistics, you probably don't equate the United States with staggering rates of infant mortality.

According to a 2018 study published in *Health Affairs*, the United States has a 76 percent higher risk of infant mortality than in nineteen other peer countries. The study compared the nation to wealthy and democratic countries such as Canada, Australia, France, Sweden, and the United Kingdom and found that the US has held this rank since the 1990s. Additionally, the infant death rate from extreme prematurity is three times other comparable countries.

Ashish Thakrar, one of the authors of the study, said, "It really seems to be the impact of our fragmented health care system. Mothers who are qualifying for Medicaid for the first time because they're mothers might be seeing doctors for the first time. They might not have a family physician, or a clear support system."

Pregnancy is a time where a woman is keenly aware of the state of their community. Throughout evolution, this stage of life is traditionally one where a tribe or community comes together to help guide the woman through birth and into becoming a parent. Child-rearing happened within a social structure that offered support to both the mother and the child. Other women, parents, relatives or friends made space for the pregnant person to talk about their fears or expectations, and provided advice and guidance.

In my experience, this looked like friends taking turns

bringing healthy meals over to the new parents, perhaps even watching the baby so the mother could relax, sleep, or take care of other responsibilities. In a crisis, someone was just a phone call away to help. If the mother had a question, there were elders or experienced mothers to connect with. Help was only a phone call away.

These are not huge gestures or expensive acts, but these seemingly small and simple gifts are one of the ways we weave the fabric of support within a community.

With the increased isolation and loneliness in our society, more and more women go through this experience alone, and feel sole responsibility for their health and their child's health. The study on infant mortality suggests that stress, especially on low-income and minority women, is compounded by the lack of social support.

In our current reality, women feel isolated, with no one to share their problems with. The support falls on healthcare professionals, who often work in environments that can't accommodate ample time and space for true care and attention.

Over two decades ago, Sharon Schindler Rising, a Yale-trained midwife, found herself constantly apologizing to patients because there wasn't enough time. Looking for a way to solve the problem, she started bringing women who were due at the same time together for prenatal care in a two-hour group visit. CenteringPregnancy® was launched.

The solution to this is not costly or technologically intensive. It is simple and elegant: gathering a group of women in a room to discuss pregnancy, answer questions, and prepare them for motherhood. It doesn't matter if it was a woman's first child or her third—either way, she was given a comfortable environment in which to talk about her experience and engage with other women going through the same thing. Yes, the curriculum is important, but like Dr. Geller realized in his first group, the curriculum is secondary to the sense of community that's fostered.

Fast forward two decades, and CenteringPregnancy now has 125 research studies and peer reviews, a 33–34 percent reduction of risk of preterm birth, and has flattened the racial differences in outcomes, as people of color previously experienced higher risks. Centering Healthcare Institute (CHI), a small nonprofit in Boston, has developed and sustained the Centering model in nearly 600 practice sites within communities in more than forty-four states, and in some of the largest health systems in the world.

One of the states that suffers the most is South Carolina, which had the forty-ninth worst infant mortality rate in

2005, second only to Mississippi, with rates similar to those in Third World countries.

In the women's clinic she runs in Greenville, South Carolina, Dr. Amy Crockett and her staff typically conducted one-on-one visits with patients to check their vitals and answer any questions they had about pregnancy and birth. She was a little skeptical that "having women sit together in a circle for their medical visits would somehow improve their birth outcomes," but decided to try it.

She applied for a grant from March of Dimes for CenteringPregnancy group prenatal care. The billable, two-hour visit is built on health assessment, interactive learning, and community building.

Around the same time Dr. Crockett launched her CenteringPregnancy program, a 2007 Yale study showed group prenatal care reduced preterm births by 29 percent overall, and 36 percent for African American women. The following year, a study in New York City showed how women who participated in group visits were less likely to have babies who were underweight or admitted to the neonatal intensive care unit (NICU).

A 2016 paper surveyed five years' worth of outcomes for the CenteringPregnancy pilot program in South Carolina, and found that it reduced the risk of premature birth by 36 percent. "For every premature birth prevented, there was an average savings of $22,667 in health expenditures." Likewise, incidents of low birth weights were reduced by 44 percent and the risk of a NICU stay was reduced by 28 percent.

Groups of parents who received their prenatal care through CenteringPregnancy demanded that they stay together as a cohort after the baby's arrival. CenteringParenting® developed organically as a way to guide new parents through "family-centered well-child care through the first two years" of the baby's life. Better health outcomes start with the mother's pregnancy, and ripple outward to impact the entire family, and eventually, the community.

Marena Burnett, Senior Director of Engagement and Innovation at Centering Healthcare Institute, reports there are now over 600 healthcare practices across the US that offer Centering, serving approximately 70,000 patients per year. They've expanded their resources beyond pregnancy and parenting, providing tools for providers who want to apply the Centering methodology to other conditions. So far, this includes diabetes, hypertension, autoimmune, and lifestyle groups.

Centering is the billable primary care visit, not an additional program or class, and can be a cost-neutral, scalable intervention. Reimbursement through Medicaid and other insurance effectively subsidizes a platform for influencing the behaviors of thousands of parents in a child's critical early years. Centering also meets the demand placed on healthcare providers as part of the shift to value-based payment, and reimbursement based on quality measures.

Dr. Geller's work and Centering are examples of setting up new communities to treat social isolation and catalyze significant shifts in health outcomes. These both speak to the range of health issues that can be solved by group visits and community, whether it's chronic or acute diseases. And in both instances, they're operating within the medical system to help change it from the inside out.

Though the system possesses the infrastructure and budget to aid in the creation of these new communities through group visits, the next obvious question becomes: If community is such a powerful mediator of disease that it works for both acute and chronic issues, how can we take advantage of preexisting communities to create health exponentially?

THE DANIEL PLAN

Groups focused on health creations can exist outside the medical system, and peer-led groups have delivered some noteworthy case studies. If we're really interested in true transformation, it can't only come from communities that are built from scratch inside the current healthcare system.

The Daniel Plan is one spectacular example of how we can tap into the power of existing communities.

Rick Warren is the pastor of Saddleback Church, a congregation of 15,000 individuals who attend services and events each week in Lake Forest, California. Struggling with his weight, and recognizing how his congregation also struggled, Pastor Warren decided to do something about it. He enlisted the help of functional medicine pioneer Dr. Mark Hyman, brain expert Dr. Daniel Amen, and heart surgeon-turned-TV star Dr. Mehmet Oz to develop a health creation curriculum with a unique twist.

In addition to big church services on Sundays, the congregation also met in small groups every Wednesday evening for Bible study. Since they already knew one another, there was already a high level of trust, and much of the community infrastructure was already in place.

This community structure proved to be the perfect place to plant the seed of new behaviors, and support one another in sticking to them. The program was an immense success: their 15,000-person congregation lost a combined 250,000 pounds.

The Daniel Plan has been turned into a *New York Times* bestselling book, and scaled to reach individuals and communities across the world. Over 200,000 people have been reached by this initiative to date, with the book translated into fourteen languages. I mentioned it in my first book as an example of how functional medicine is superbly positioned to be a leader in the convergence of community and medicine.

Centering and Dr. Geller both operate within the medical system. But with The Daniel Plan, we see the transformative power of groups being disintermediated from the disease care system, which was really never created with lifestyle-driven chronic disease care in mind.

One of the things I argued in the *Evolution of Medicine* is how difficult it is for the disease care system to adapt to health creation, because our current healthcare paradigm was created in an era of pathogenesis. Everything in medicine was created around disease: billing codes, which practitioners you see in which order, diagnostics. What's been done in The Daniel Plan, with Dr. Geller, and Centering is based on a completely different model: salutogenesis.

Sociologist and professor Aaron Antonovsky coined the

term "salutogenesis" in 1979, but it was only just added to the Merriam-Webster dictionary in 2019. Rooted in the Latin *salus*, or health, and the Greek *genesis*, or origin, the term encompasses all aspects of health creation and acts as a contrast to the disease care approach. Antonovsky wanted a word to summarize the origins of health, as his research focused on the role of culture in shaping health and well-being.

Traditionally, the family unit was a structure where health could flourish. I've seen countless examples over the years of how a child's illness leads to lifestyle changes for the whole family, then affecting other parents, the school, or other members of the community. Alternatively, unhealthy habits travel through friend groups and families, so much so that if a child is obese, there is a 40 percent higher risk of obesity in their siblings, according to the *British Journal of Sports Medicine*.

Where community already exists—whether in families, schools, offices, factories, campuses, prisons, senior living facilities, or churches—we have an opportunity to build a new culture of health.

Emerging solutions to chronic illness need to be based on a salutogenic theory, which demands new paradigms that consider the interaction of biological, psychological, and social factors in a biopsychosocial approach.

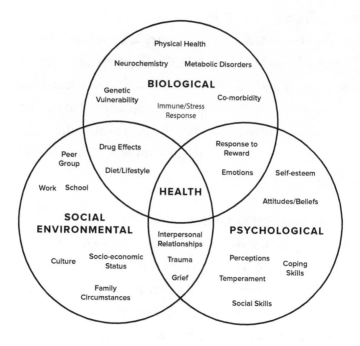

First proposed by George L. Engel and John Romano of Rochester University in 1977, the biopsychosocial model sets out a more holistic view for both illnesses and psychological issues. It was far ahead of its time, seeing the development of illness through the complex interaction of biological (genetic, biochemical), social (community, relationships), and psychological (personality, mood) factors. Over the last forty years, we have learned so much more about human physiology that only reinforces their thesis, most notably systems biology, the microbiome and epigenetics—the science of how environmental factors turn on and off genes.

The group visit is unique in its ability to treat each of these three aspects—biological, social and psychological—simultaneously, with a synergistic effect.

Imagine an unfortunately prevalent situation in our world: where social isolation triggers an underlying genetic predisposition that leads to depression. We can see how this becomes a vicious cycle—a social factor, affecting a biological mechanism, and leading to a psychological diagnosis.

In the same way, imagine someone attending a group. By learning to trust again, the body is sent the signal of safety, and epigenetics kicks in and depression is lifted, such is the majesty of the human body. A truly virtuous circle. Now, all we have to do is deal with the psychotropic drug dependence (which we'll discuss in chapter seven).

A biological input can't solve a biopsychosocial problem. But that won't stop pharmaceutical-funded academia from trying.

Researchers at the University of Chicago are developing a pill to treat loneliness. Yes, you heard that right. Yet Julianne Holt-Kunstad—a psychology professor at Brigham Young University and one of the authors of a paper on social isolation and loneliness—told *Smithsonian* that a pill, though helpful, would be best-served if physicians and healthcare professionals had additional methods to deal with loneliness.

"Being socially connected needs to be seen as much a part of a healthy lifestyle as eating right and exercising." Holt-Kundstad asks, "How do we better equip people to start thinking about this as part of their healthier lifestyle?"

The rise in interest in functional medicine comes on the back of a realization that a "pill for every ill" model doesn't work for chronic illness, which couldn't be clearer here.

Through the lens of the biopsychosocial model it makes sense that complex chronic illness benefits from delivering care in a group setting. Not only is the community powerful enough to deal with the social stress of isolation, it is also a place where the fundamentals of health creation—diet, exercise, stress management, sleep, all of which significantly impact the biological and psychological aspects—are able to be both developed and sustained. Therefore, groups must form the bedrock of the evolution of medicine.

CHAPTER TWO

THE DOUBTS

"The fundamental cause of the trouble is that in the modern world the stupid are cocksure while the intelligent are full of doubt."

—BERTRAND RUSSELL

If you are reading this, it's likely that this isn't the first time you have seen or heard about the concept of people healing in groups. It has been successfully utilized as a mechanism for addiction recovery in models like Alcoholics Anonymous since 1935. In 1991, Dr. John C. Scott implemented a group visit model at the Cooperative Health Care Clinic with Kaiser Colorado staff because he was frustrated with the lack of quality time spent with patients. In 1996, Dr. Edward Noffsinger launched the Drop-In Group Medical Appointment (DIGMA) while at Kaiser Permanente in California, and published *Running Group Visits in Your Practice* in 2009 as a guide for other physicians.

Over the last six years, I've spoken to thousands of doctors and practitioners about group visits. A range of doubts and objections come up. Some are skeptical about the efficacy of them, or their own ability to run them. Many are just so burned out that the idea of trying anything new seems really overwhelming.

There is one concern that always seems to come up first and so I want to deal with it up front. You might call it "The Elephant in the Group Visit Room."

PRIVACY

The biggest question people have about group medicine is privacy.

The Hippocratic Oath was written in Greek in roughly 400 BC, and became the foundation for modern patient privacy guidelines. In one translation, it reads, "What I may see or hear in the course of the treatment or even outside of the treatment in regard to the life of men, which on no account one must spread abroad, I will keep to myself, holding such things shameful to be spoken about."

The intention behind it is noble: that physicians should keep patient information to themselves, honoring the person's privacy. But in the thesaurus, one synonym of privacy is isolation. It's absurd to think that we're going to be able to solve social isolation with the very thing that contributes to it.

We're experiencing the highest rates of chronic disease in history, and it's time to reconsider what brought us here.

What I find interesting is the mention of shame, and its association with disease or treatment. Many people suffering from chronic illness find it difficult to discuss with others because of that exact emotion. Shame is born of feelings of inadequacy, unworthiness, dishonor and regret, and ultimately disconnection.

This doesn't just apply to chronic illness either. In the last chapter, we talked about how CenteringPregnancy is drastically improving rates of preterm births and NICU admissions simply by gathering women in a room. When we as a community or society isolate women in this phase of life, the outcomes speak for themselves. In a certain way, privacy is the opposite of what these women need, and the impact of CenteringPregnancy clearly shows the importance of community.

Thankfully, group visits don't destroy patient privacy.

People are welcome to share as they feel comfortable within the group, and they still have access to one-on-one care if they need to discuss something confidential.

As you'll see in later chapters, many of the models that are billed to insurance include semi-private micro-consultations with practitioners, where specific issues can be discussed and addressed. In chapter six, we'll walk through how to craft agreements and expectations surrounding privacy and confidentiality, which builds trust among participants.

We often associate privacy with protection. It shelters us. We need to find a balance between being private and being open.

By connecting individuals who are going through the same experience, we offer a safe space in which to be vulnerable. In doing so, they learn how to trust and rely on one another for support. This is often what keeps participants coming back, and what some say they'll miss the most when a group is over. In some circumstances, people become closer within the group than they are with their own families. Unfortunately, openness is not a societal norm—one we're not taught in school or in our own families.

The need for privacy in certain situations is important, but the vast majority of issues plaguing us today need to be brought out into the light. We need more connection, more empathy, more social connectivity, and less loneliness, less social isolation. In a culture and society that emphasizes or prioritizes privacy, we're inadvertently contributing to the very epidemic we're trying to solve.

If privacy is the reason you haven't implemented group visits, it's time to fundamentally reconsider the role of privacy in our lives and health. Fortunately, or not, it comes at a time where all of us—individually and as a society—are looking at this exact topic in light of the ongoing social media and data breach scandals. It's nonsensical to freely give away all your data to big tech like Google or Facebook so they can turn around and sell you things, but at the same time to be hyper concerned about other data and how it travels within groups of people sitting in a room together—people who are much more likely to have your best interests at heart.

As we shift society from what Charles Eisenstein calls the "age of separation" to an "age of interbeing," the stories we tell ourselves must be open for change. Once we get comfortable with the new reality of privacy and openness, the next doubt that arises is whether or not this actually works.

CAN GROUP VISITS REALLY IMPACT HEALTH OUTCOMES?

An exemplary model of a system that is realizing the potential of group visits is the Cleveland Clinic Center for Functional Medicine (CCCFM). It's the first clinic in the United States to have a functional medicine practice within a major academic medical center. Dr. Mark Hyman announced the start of the center on the fourth episode of the Functional Forum in May 2014, and we've been following its evolution ever since, as an example of medicine adapting to its environment. Since then, the center has gone through a transformation that shows the way forward.

Tawny Jones is the CCCFM's chief administrator tasked with clinic operations, strategic planning, and expanding the functional medicine care model throughout the organization. She's worked for the Cleveland Clinic for almost twenty years as an energetic advocate for health creation.

On the *Evolution of Medicine* podcast in 2019, Jones said CCCFM's goal, "is to truly transform healthcare by empowering patients to take control of their health."

Since CCCFM opened in October 2014, 12,100 patients from forty-eight states and thirty-three countries have sought out their services. The reputation of the Cleveland Clinic, when combined with the systems-based patient care model of functional medicine, had people clambering to access it. In 2016, Jones said there were nearly 2,000 patients trying to see the five physicians they had on staff. The waitlist was twelve to eighteen months.

"The math simply didn't work. We were at this critical juncture where patients were outnumbering the providers at a pace that wasn't even manageable."

Around the same time, CCCFM launched The Daniel Plan, discussed in the first chapter, working with Pastor Rick Warren to establish the faith-based wellness program in a dozen churches in Cleveland. Clinicians partnered with the organization to bring small groups together for six weeks, and saw great results with weight loss, lowered blood pressure, and less reliance on medications. Through this, CCCFM witnessed the value and impact of a group model.

In her car on the way to work, Jones asked herself, "How do we bring the essence of functional medicine to a group model and include the components of nutrition and health coaching in a way that leads to sustainable behavior change?" She envisioned delivering "this program in a systematic way that would teach patients to move from surviving with their chronic condition to thriving and functioning for life."

From that brainstorming session on her commute, Functioning for Life™ was born: a ten-week patient experience to address common conditions like weight management, diabetes, autoimmune and digestive disorders, pain, and women's health.

Physicians worked to create a program that would ensure that by the end of the ten weeks, participants possessed "this full toolbox for their health that included everything they needed and should know about self-management of their condition." This included fourteen hours of curriculum from a dietician, health coach, physician or physician assistant or nurse practitioner, who teaches them about a whole foods diet, the effects of nutritional deficiencies on their health, stress management, relaxation techniques, healthy sleeping patterns, and the power of movement. Patients learned how to interpret their own labs, and understand how to improve or shift their results.

It breaks down biopsychosocial root causes into a manageable, motivating ten-week system, one in which they have the power to make changes. They're no longer relying on a provider to "fix" them. For some patients, these ten weeks are just the beginning.

"It doesn't matter how long it takes a patient to make a change in their health as long as we encourage them to never stop trying," Jones said. "We don't give up on them. We might switch our message with how we're working with them individually, but we never switch our goal of helping them reach theirs."

Functioning for Life is "the intersection between medical management and social connection." As Jones notes, "people are tired of being handed a treatment plan without an execution plan," or "an after-visit summary that doesn't teach them or provide the tools for them to successfully manage their disease [and] doesn't help them move the needle forward."

Functioning for Life launched in March of 2017, and by 2019 they had guided 1,000 patients through the program. Eighty percent of patients attend every appointment, which is an excellent retention rate. CCCFM also tracks outcomes using the Patient-Reported Outcomes Measurement Information System (PROMIS), "a National Institute of Health-validated tool for measuring physical, mental, and social health of individuals with chronic disease." Previously, Dr. Hyman noted that moving the needle forward even one point in the PROMIS scores is difficult in the short term, but Jones notes that 40 percent of Functioning for Life patients experience a five-point or higher improvement in their scores.

"The preliminary findings definitely demonstrate that this model of care truly improves our patients' health-related quality of life." The success is attributed to both the functional medicine approach and "the social connection that happens between the patients."

According to Dr. Hyman, about half of the people who went through the Functioning for Life curriculum didn't need to see a doctor at the end of ten weeks. CCCFM was able to address the issue of the twelve- to eighteen-month waitlist, utilize physician assistants, health coaches, and other providers, who could all help empower patients.

This is incredible given the depth of care these individuals needed when they started—people who had seen multiple specialists and sometimes depended on dozens of medications. Even though there are different treatment options available, Tawny Jones said many patients "opt into various programs because they want that group connection. They want that support system. They want that advocacy that happens within the group model."

These aren't individuals who are exceptionally forthcoming about their struggles with chronic disease or used to advocating for themselves. These patients are "really reticent about sharing their health issues," due in part to the social stigma associated with disease and low self-confidence. Halfway through the ten-week program, Jones says, "they find their voice, they're empowered, the feeling of loneliness dissipates, they're developing relationships, and they're encouraging each other to go on." Thirty percent of individuals are referred to the program by a friend or family member that has gone through it, showing they're happy enough with results to recommend it to others. Every few months, CCCFM holds a Functioning for Life Reunion so patients can share their personal stories, accomplishments, and progress with the community. This is great for the participants but also for the providers, who have the chance to actually see the positive results of their work in real-time, thereby motivating them to continue, and showing them new possibilities for group medicine.

For those who doubt the efficacy of the group model, the Cleveland Clinic's Functioning for Life program serves as an exemplary model, one that Tawny Jones touts as a game changer for healthcare.

"In an era where we're looking for high-quality, cost-effective means of delivering sustainable behavior change in patients, and reversing chronic disease, and lowering overall healthcare costs, you need programs like this."

As of January 2020, the Cleveland Clinic is now offering training in the Functioning for Life model, not only in Cleveland for individual clinicians and small practice groups, but also traveling to other medical centers to train whole departments. (We'll discuss other existing group programs in chapter six, and you can visit goevomed.com/groups for more information.)

In my last book, physicians were at the forefront of the evolution of medicine, building low overhead, functional medicine practices. Now, with the convergence of community and medicine, everyone can take part, from administrators to midwives and everyone in between. It's not solely on the shoulders of physicians to deliver group medicine, and Tawny Jones shows us how even administrators see the immense value and potential of group visits—even addressing the previously vexing problem of profitability.

WILL PRACTICING GROUP VISITS MAKE MONEY?

For almost a decade now, I have been helping doctors, health professionals, and small group practices adapt their clinics to the new realities of treating lifestyle-driven chronic illness. This puts me in a position to have some very honest conversations with decision-makers in practices, and for some of them, one doubt about running group visits has been the nuts and bolts of finances.

This is particularly sensitive for practitioners delivering integrative and functional medicine. Not only do doctors choosing to practice in this way more often than not make less money than their colleagues, it has been even harder to make ends meet at the institutional level. Since 2015, a number of the most prominent integrative centers in the country, like the Continuum Center in New York, have shut down for economic reasons.

Despite being called the "crown jewel" of Beth Israel, bringing a high percentage of new patients to the system and getting consistently great reviews, in 2017 the center was shut down as, after a merger, Mt. Sinai started to take a more limited view of how to assess value, focused on relative value units (RVUs).

When you take a step back, the math is pretty simple: you can make more money per square foot putting in heart stents than you can coaching people to change their diets one on one.

For CCCFM, group medicine has proved to be more profitable than individualized visits, which are time-intensive and reliant on physicians. With a group visit, the clinic bills multiple people's insurance for the same appointment and utilizes other staff or lower-cost providers, leading to a highly profitable model.

As you'll hear in later chapters, the group visit model has proven profitable and sustainable for a range of organizations. Some are able to offer it to Medicaid and Medicare patients. In private practice, billing multiple insurances works out favorably, and there are even options to implement a cash model that radically simplifies administration and makes both provider and patients happy.

Throughout this book, you'll see examples of how group-delivered services have saved significant amounts of money for organizations when compared to one-on-one care. At a macro level, saving money is a fiscal imperative. However, each healthcare organization has different incentives. Saving money might be more interesting to self-funded employers or governments, while most American healthcare organizations (like hospitals, clinics, practice groups, and even insurance groups) don't want to save money, they want to make money.

Group visits offer the best of both worlds: if your organization wants to save money, it can save money by creating self efficacy in patients, weaning them off medication, and keeping them out of the emergency room.

If your organization wants to make money, it can make money by billing multiple users for the same service, while only paying one or two practitioners to run the groups. It has the unique advantage of being both accessible and profitable.

Everyone in healthcare knows one thing: incentives matter. One of the most significant changes in the way healthcare is being paid for is the shift from fee-for-service to fee-for-value. This shift, especially in America, has been very slow to materialize until now. If there is one thing all the group visit leaders agree on, it is this: once everyone starts getting paid to keep people well, as opposed to delivering discrete services, group visits will be a big winner.

ARE INDIVIDUALIZED MEDICINE AND GROUPS MUTUALLY EXCLUSIVE?

In my first book I wanted to awaken physicians to the possibilities of realizing the aspiration of P4 medicine—personalized, predictive, preventive, and participatory—with the operating system of functional medicine. If you're currently a functional medicine practitioner, or a patient of one, you're probably deeply entrenched in the ideology that individualized medicine is the best approach.

Over the last one hundred years, physicians heavily relied on science and research to determine what was the best approach for each condition. As new solutions, typically medication, were developed, they were tested over a population, and—if it was proven beneficial—introduced to the marketplace as the standard of care. This was exceptional at discovering what was the best solution for the average human, but as time has gone on, many forward-thinking physicians and frustrated patients have started to wonder if an average human actually exists.

If your curiosity was piqued by the biopsychosocial model, then this next graphic might be the knockout punch for "medicine for the average."

In 2015, an article in *Nature* reported significant findings: expensive prescriptions really weren't working for most people. As you can see from the graph below, out of the top ten drugs in America (by dollar value), for every one person that was helped by Humira, an autoimmune biological, three received no benefit. For Nexium, the result was one to twenty-four.

Not only are they not working, they're also creating side effects that patients then need to cope with using other methods, whether that's supplements, lifestyle changes, or more often than not, further prescriptions.

Imprecision Medicine

For every person they do help (black), the ten highest-grossing drugs in the United States fail to improve the conditions of between 3 and 24 people (white)

1. ABILIFY (aripiprazole)
Schizophrenia

👤👤👤
👤👤

2. NEXIUM (esomeprazole)
Erosive Esophagitis

👤👤👤👤👤👤👤👤👤👤👤
👤👤👤👤👤👤👤👤👤👤👤

3. HUMIRA (adalimumab)
Arthritis

👤👤
👤👤

4. CRESTOR (rosuvastatin)
Primary prevention of cardiovascular events

👤👤👤👤👤👤👤👤👤
👤👤👤👤👤👤👤👤👤

5. CYMBALTA (duloxetine)
Depression

👤👤👤👤👤
👤👤👤👤

6. ADVAIR DISKUS (fluticasone/salmeterol)
COPD exacerbation

👤👤👤👤👤👤👤👤👤👤
👤👤👤👤👤👤👤👤👤👤

7. ENBREL (etanercept)
Arthritis

👤👤
👤👤

8. REMICADE (infliximab)
Arthritis

👤👤
👤👤

9. COPAXONE (glatiramer acetate)
Multiple Sclerosis

👤👤👤👤👤👤👤
👤👤👤👤👤👤👤

9. NEULASTA (pegfilgrastim)
Infections after stem cell transplant

👤👤👤👤👤👤
👤👤👤👤👤

Based on published number needed to treat (NNT) figures. For a full list of references, see Supplementary Information at go.nature.com/4dr78f.

Dr. Jeffrey Bland, the godfather of functional medicine and my cohost on *The Big Bold Health Podcast*, said in a 2017 keynote that we've thought about "health as an aggregate to disease." Once you're diagnosed with that disease, you're placed into a class and treated the same as everyone else who also has the same disease.

"What we've recognized now through genomic science, is that is actually not true. If you look at any specific one of these chronic diseases that are commonplace in our culture now, what you will find is that people with the same disease have very different patterns of genetic expression that result in those diseases."

Dr. Bland added that this explains why treatments fail and patients have adverse reactions. With genetics and epigenetics, we're now seeing that people who have the same disease can sometimes be more dissimilar than they are similar. Even though they're receiving the same treatments or drugs as everyone else with this disease, the effectiveness ranges significantly.

The *Nature* article reinforced one thing to me, conventional medicine just isn't working for most people with chronic illness. The drug plan isn't sufficient for the kind of health outcomes patients deserve and desire. It's these kinds of statistics and results that are prompting a shift to lifestyle-first, root-cause approaches like functional medicine.

Dr. Bland has called for a move away from the era of the average and toward the era of the individual, meaning that some people have actually moved away from a disease label-based approach in order to treat each person individually.

So does that mean that group visits are dead in the era of personalized medicine?

Quite the opposite.

Although personalized medicine is important, ultimately it can only be practiced by those empowered to participate. For people who are disempowered, individualized medicine is a fairytale.

VISION: PRECISION PUBLIC HEALTH

Dr. Jeffrey Geller defines empowerment as "the ability to try new things," which often "comes from support." This means having the time and resources to test new treatments or lifestyle changes, and having a support system or community that will hold you accountable and validate these shifts. Personalized medicine makes sense for this population, many of whom are already on board with functional medicine.

The vast majority of people are not in an empowered state. In America, some avoid going to the doctor because of copays or lack of insurance coverage. They don't get the diagnosis because it means taking action on it, which they may not be able to afford, don't have the time to implement treatment plans, or don't have the resources and support systems they need for their own care. This includes the ability to take time off work for appointments, and having reliable transportation to get there. There can even be a certain degree of shame or embarrassment that comes with a diagnosis, making people feel more alone in their struggle. A disempowered individual might not be ready to read and interpret their own labs, but you can see in the Cleveland Clinic example that empowerment can happen rapidly when the conditions and support is right.

How can the medical system empower people to take their health into their own hands? One solution is to put people in a room to connect and discuss it together, empowering one another in the process.

When I saw Dr. Geller model his empowerment group visit in person at the Integrative Medicine for the Underserved conference, I saw what it really amounts to: being a conduit for groups of disempowered people to work together to solve *their own problems* dynamically. This can be as simple as providing transportation for one another if one participant doesn't have a car. Hey, you can even drive in the HOV lane together!

As you'll see later in the book, groups don't negate the

potential for individualized solutions. In our Practice Accelerator, we've seen physicians innovate around the delivery of personalized medicine. One of the ways to do this is to utilize the efficiency of a group setting to help patients chart their individual health histories together, understand lab testing and values, and more. It's satisfying for patients to learn in groups, and much more efficient for the provider.

When the patients outnumber the practitioner, there's a sense of safety and belonging. They're not the only one in the room with a diagnosis, an issue, or a struggle. Other people have the same feelings, questions, and concerns. With group medicine, it's possible to elevate disempowered communities into an empowered state, while also leaving space for individualized care.

Personalized medicine and group-delivered care are not mutually exclusive; they are both necessary to actualize an emerging vision of "precision public health." As access to genetic information becomes ever easier and cheaper, and other forms of technology like biometric tracking even more ubiquitous, it is clear that personalized medicine is the next evolution in medical care. The only remaining question is how we will get there.

Precision medicine is about "delivering the right treatments, at the right time, every time to the right person," according to former President Obama. Precision public health extends this concept to entire populations, but if the majority of Americans are not sufficiently empowered to participate, this concept is difficult to actualize. The path to precision public health is not a prescription pill.

As you will see in the next chapter, there is enough data to suggest that group visits by themselves are largely effective for solving certain social determinants of health—specifically community and social context, nutrition, education, and access to care—by creating self-efficacy and allowing people the power to participate in their care. So what should they do with this newfound empowerment?

Functional medicine is an operating system for delivering personalized medicine. By helping individuals first truly understand their own health history, they begin to understand themselves as unique. By learning how the body breaks down through long-term environmental inputs, they start to see their health through the lens of function. In discovering their distinct sensitivities with low-cost tools like elimination diets, we have built a foundation for personalized medicine for everyone. This operating system, which was previously too time intensive or costly for most physicians, can be elegantly executed in a group format.

But the beauty is in connecting the two into a new layer of primary care that sits between society and the current medical system. The synergy of these two emerging trends is both effective and affordable enough to become a new standard of care, minimizing costs and maximizing healthspan.

CHAPTER THREE

THE MENTORS

"Mentorship brings out the latent qualities within us that are sometimes hard to realize without support."

—RUSSELL BRAND

The first time I heard about group visits was at a Conference in 2013 called Heal Thy Practice. There, Dr. Shilpa Saxena described her disillusionment with the pill-for-every-ill model of dealing with chronic illness, which drove her to look for alternatives. From her initial training in family medicine, she made the shift toward functional, integrative, and lifestyle medicine, eventually becoming a faculty member at the Institute for Functional Medicine and at George Washington University's Metabolic Medicine Institute, plus a fellow and guest faculty at the Arizona Center for Integrative Medicine, and a volunteer assistant professor of family medicine and community health at the University of Miami's Miller School of Medicine.

Dr. Saxena was beyond busy. She had two young children at home. Her practice in Lutz, Florida, began to grow. As it did, the short allotments of time she had with patients wasn't nearly enough to express everything she needed to teach them to address the root causes of their ailments.

The tipping point was when her physician assistant left on maternity leave. Dr. Saxena found herself solely responsible for seeing 4,000 patients.

Necessity is the mother of all invention. She knew she couldn't be the only physician with this problem, so she researched new models of care and found Dr. Edward Noffsinger's work, who launched the Drop-In Group Medical Appointment (DIGMA) in 1996.

Adapting the conventional DIGMA framework as a time-saving tool, Dr. Shilpa Saxena created a new model in 2008, one that combined it with functional medicine. For the next three months, she brought together patients who either had the same diagnosis, like diabetes or osteoporosis, or could benefit from the same information, like how to do an elimination diet or address high blood pressure.

Instead of individual appointments, where she maybe had five minutes with a patient, she could spend ninety minutes with sixteen people. There was more time for teaching meaningful content, as opposed to just sending someone home with a handout. It was incredibly efficient, as she often repeated the same information in individual appointments anyway.

Patients want more time with physicians, and physicians want more time with patients. But the piece that's often forgotten is that patients also want time with other patients. "Social health is key," Dr. Saxena said, "and you just cannot get that on a one-to-one appointment."

In individual appointments, patients didn't always know what questions to ask. Later, they'd call the clinic to ask, thereby creating more work for the staff. In the group visits, Dr. Saxena and her staff witnessed how the room full of people with the same diagnosis would brainstorm and ask questions together.

"There's a unique power of self-efficacy that comes into each one of those patients because now they have this group of peers." Combining the power of one's peers with the right information leads to empowerment, and the transition from just knowing the information to actually acting on the information.

"Knowing is not equal to doing," Dr. Saxena said, "and that is where the magic of group visits is, because there are some dynamics that occur when people come together for a shared goal, and they get to share their struggles."

In her two-practitioner model, there was one billable provider (Dr. Saxena) and one non-billable provider, a health coach, to support and educate the group. For the first time, I saw how all of the issues that have prevented the widespread adoption of a lifestyle-focused approach to medicine were solved with one elegant solution.

In the past, physicians struggled to support a patient's lifestyle changes, but the accountability of the group made it easier and took the burden off the physician. Issues with profitability were resolved, and functional medicine practices who were forced into adopting a cash model could now bill insurance for group visits. The amount of time practitioners could spend with patients allowed them to get to the root cause of people's chronic conditions without sacrificing the financial viability of their practice.

Unlike most physicians, Dr. Saxena wasn't afraid to try new things. She actually had to—she had little to no time to care for 4,000 patients, most of whom had chronic complex diseases in need of regular follow-up visits. But as she shared her new successes with the group model, she realized that many practitioners did not have the tools to operationalize this model.

What she realized—again—is that knowing isn't the same as doing, even when it came to providers. They, too, needed information and a workshop-like experience to adopt new and useful behaviors. Out of this realization, the Group Visit Toolkits were born: a package of resources that any doctor, practice, or health system could use to get up and running with group visits quickly. The resources include presentations and videos, best practices for billing insurance, group-adapted SOAP notes for efficient charting and much more. This has since expanded to include a number of specialties like digestive disorders, cardiometabolic disease, and chronic pain.

The toolkits are supported by the Lifestyle Matrix Resource Center, which helps practitioners in the early stages of adopting the new model. Before this support was available, it was seemingly daunting to transition to group medicine. Others claimed it was too hard to adopt, but this solution made it so much easier.

In her lecture, Dr. Saxena described how healthcare is lacking in both health and care. Her lifestyle-based group visit model was a win for the entire stakeholder community: patients, providers, staff, payors, employers, and society at large.

I'd seen models like group acupuncture and chiropractic offices with open treatment rooms, which were interesting but didn't go far enough—it was meant for efficiency, not connection. When I first heard Dr. Saxena speak, I sat back and thought, "This is the future of medicine." Not only because it allowed the physician to spend more time with the patient, but because the community itself was providing the majority of the value.

COMING HOME

I recognized this as the future of medicine because it was how I was raised. Until age eleven, I lived in intentional communities across the globe. Each summer, I stayed on the same 400-acre ranch in Northern Colorado where I was born, which hosted an organic farm and spiritual retreat center. The rest of the year, my family and I moved among the other locations in England and South Africa.

When I turned eleven, my father left the community abruptly and I was deposited into a different community altogether: boarding school in England.

I'm not sure if there will ever be enough teenagers who have made that particular transition for me to have a group of my peers to discuss it with. I did try—I have one very specific, vivid memory of a religious studies class when I was thirteen.

The school I went to was Anglican, otherwise known as the Church of England, which is basically Catholicism, except the Queen is the Pope. I remember venturing that I had been brought up in a community and being initially laughed out of the room, and subsequently bullied aggressively for years. I guess I didn't realize just how weird or abnormal it was and I learned pretty quickly that it was not something to talk about. My classmates had family relatives and maybe a church community, but they didn't have the extended network of other children and adults that I had growing up. I didn't speak about my experiences again with peers for almost twenty years.

Though it was ahead of its time then, the beliefs and values of the community shared much in common with contemporary self-help and spirituality. Personal accountability and a respect for nature were among core values, and they believed each person was uniquely divine and their purpose in life is to simply be their authentic selves. The spiritual practices included prayer, some chanting and a type of energy healing similar to reiki, called attunement.

The healthcare was different too. I saw a chiropractor from a young age, and the first port of call for most things in my family were homeopathic remedies. Once I was sent to boarding school, I was the only kid in school whose mother insisted they not be given antibiotics unless she approved it. Somehow, with no medical training, she had predicted the downside of overuse of antibiotics by almost thirty years. To be fair, she was surrounded by many forward-thinking doctors who joined the community in the early days of the integrative medicine movement.

Similar to many kids, I rebelled against my parents' beliefs and took a more conventional track as soon as I could. I studied economics at university, specifically health economics: the trajectory of the field and the cost of chronic conditions. The World Economic Forum estimates chronic disease will cost $47 trillion and may be the biggest impediment to long-term economic growth. I became acutely aware of the situation but brushed it aside in favor of landing the highest-paying job I could, as an investment banker.

Shortly after I started, I had a moment of clarity where I realized I was either an investment banker with an unconventional background, or perhaps my childhood had given me a unique opportunity to understand what it would take to solve one of the world's most vexing problems: chronic disease.

As long as people were taking more and more medication, the cost could never go down. I realized that the solution lay in finding ways to get people off medication and to a foundational state of health. That insight alone was enough to make me quit my high-paying job and move to America in 2005.

I spent the next eight years on the front lines, working in a clinic practicing this new standard of care and then serving doctors across the Northeast doing the same. I put 100,000 miles on my car, visited every small town from Virginia to Maine, and had more than a thousand experiences with these emerging clinic models.

The doctors I worked with didn't have a wide enough reach to make a meaningful impact. It was difficult to change deeply ingrained behaviors with a one-hour visit each month, and only a small percentage of people would see results with that architecture of support. Helping the richest 15 percent of the nation who could access this model could never solve this problem either.

All that changed when I heard Dr. Saxena speak. She was able to bill to insurance, and it was profitable because she could bill sixteen people's insurance simultaneously. The level of care and outcomes were better than most one-on-one visits. She had already developed resources for other doctors to implement the same system, taking the guesswork out of how to create and run a curriculum. All of the barriers that had been set up were knocked down by her Group Visit Toolkit.

As Dr. Saxena spoke, I realized the combination of community, something I grew up in and took for granted, and this new standard of care was the way forward.

In fact, I didn't realize it.

I knew it.

After her talk, I had the opportunity to spend time with her and we have become great friends in the years since. In 2015, she and I sat next to each other in the back row at the Institute for Functional Medicine's Annual International Conference and listened to Dr. George Slavich of the UCLA Stress Lab introduce us to the emerging field of *human social genomics*. The reason this is a new science is because only recently has technology become affordable enough to see how external inputs affect the body at the level of gene expression. As mentioned in the introduction, in that lecture he outlined how social stress and isolation was the biggest driver of all causes of mortality, more so than smoking, lack of exercise, or poor nutrition.

Dr. Saxena and I sat there in reverent silence, mixed with bursts of furious note taking. Here was the mechanism of action that explained, on a microscopic level, the importance and impact of her work, and reinforces the tremendous power of isolation to create disease, or community to create health. Ever since I've been on a mission to understand it all: the mechanism, the science, the leaders and all the ways that community can affect behavior toward healthier outcomes for all.

THE POWER OF RITUAL

Before the 1990s the majority of science on the placebo effect was only as foils to "real drugs." Every drug trial had a placebo control group and that provided a lot of insight into the scale and consistency of the effect. In the last twenty years, however, this has changed as researchers look toward not *if* the placebo effect works, but *how*.

Twenty years ago Ted Kapchuk and his fellow researchers at Harvard started to dig deeper, asking how to maximize not the effect of a drug, but the placebo effect itself. Disregarding the knowledge that placebo treatments can affect certain ailments, Kaptchuk says, "is like ignoring a huge chunk of healthcare." As caregivers, "we should be using every tool in the box."

In the early 2000s Kapchuk got his first opportunity to test different placebos against each other, and was the first to uncover a "dose-dependent response" for placebo, showing essentially that more care equaled a higher placebo response rate. The more the doctor engaged patients in the therapeutic encounter, the greater the effect.

Since then the research has gone to the next level, showing the placebo effect can work even when patients know it is a placebo, understanding the neural mechanism of action as well at the nocebo response.

In his book *How Healing Works,* Dr. Wayne Jonas examined the stories of patients who healed unexpectedly. What he found was similar to what most physicians refer to as the placebo response: when a person who is ill perceives or experiences improvements just from the psychological effect of receiving treatment, as opposed to the treatment itself.

But instead of the placebo effect causing the outcome, Dr. Jonas reframed it as the "ritual effect."

Dr. Jonas is a retired Lieutenant Colonel in the Medical Corps of the US Army and the former Director of the Office of Alternative Medicine at the National Institutes of Health, who then went on to launch and run the Samueli Institute, a nonprofit research organization.

In his research and book, he reframes the idea of the placebo effect to highlight the power and importance of ritual. The ritual of a doctor in a white coat giving you a pill that would supposedly heal you was an act that triggered this effect. Traditionally, communities regularly gathered for daily or weekly rituals, whether that was mealtimes, religious or spiritual services, or assemblies. Elders offered advice, wisdom, knowledge, and counseling based on their experience and what was passed down to them. Many coming-of-age rituals were about vulnerability and building self-reliance.

The most elaborate and consistent ritual we have as a species, in humanity, is to come together in a circle.

This is not a new idea that we're asking the medical system to create from scratch. It's a return to ancient ideas that have stood the test of time, most notably in indigenous cultures. In researching this book I spoke to Iron Eagle of the Yankton Sioux Tribe of South Dakota, who shared the theme of the circle in daily grounding rituals and communal ceremonies. These meetings tapped into the power of the collective to heal through ritual, sound, and healing techniques through herbal medicine. It's understood that every human desires acceptance, belonging, to be part of a group. We're at a time in history where it's imperative to "reenergize the circle."

This goes against our current culture's obsession with privacy, which we addressed in the last chapter. Dr. Jonas notes that patients ultimately don't care where the treatment comes from, as long as it's effective. Pharmaceutical science wants the treatment to work and not the placebo, because they can then turn around and sell the products. Yet in *How Healing Works*, Dr. Jonas writes about how the unintended consequences of treatments might outweigh the benefits of the drug itself.

Even proven treatments that target specific molecular pathways and so create their intended effects usually have effects on unintended targets producing unwanted side effects. Thus, the very treatments that work, those producing the benefits seen in 20-30 percent in randomized studies also produced unwanted effects. Those unwanted effects frequently impact 50-70 percent of those who take them, including when the treatment did not work. In short, complex systems like the human body, specific treatments have a higher probability of causing harm than good. Judging whether these harms are worth the benefits challenge all of us in medicine.

What Dr. Jonas advocates for in his book is a shift to whole system science, bringing the entire mind and body into balance, and building resilience. This requires looking at the whole person. Though this may sound complex, it's going to take complex solutions to solve complex problems.

Thankfully, this doesn't have to be complicated. The body is its own intricate system, and the effects of a simple intervention, like exercise or healthy eating, benefits that system in complex ways. Practicing healthy behaviors in supportive social environments multiplies those positive effects.

Furthermore, when I asked Dr. Jonas about his thoughts on group visits, he was extremely bullish. "A group visit is like having fifteen unpaid health coaches supporting you on your journey to health." If the greater attention from your health professional can induce a larger placebo response, then what can the exquisite attention of fifteen people do?

Research like Dr. Jonas's is why a growing number of people now disagree with the single therapeutic drug approach to treating complex chronic disease. They are well suited for acute issues with one identifiable cause, but it's an inappropriate intervention to treat chronic disease—especially when we start treating the side effects with further medication.

But if we really want to change the direction of healthcare and get the doctors, clinics, health systems, and even sovereign nations to take on this approach, we need to have solid science to prove it works.

CATALOGUING THE SCIENCE

Early on, Dr. Paula Gardiner had inklings that group settings were conducive to learning. As the daughter of a minister, she'd seen the power of community firsthand. Just after college, she engaged in mindfulness-based stress reduction courses and found it much easier to practice in a group. Fresh out of medical school, as a resident in family medicine at Tufts, her first project was to run a medical group visit for patients with diabetes. She then did a fellowship at Harvard, where she investigated how to deliver integrative medicine in a group setting.

"What it allowed us to do," she said, "is to bring techniques, services, and different ideas that were not accessible to low-income patients." Previously, in her experiences at the Boston Medical Center, she witnessed how low-income patient populations in tertiary medical care settings were really only given the option of prescriptions: "In our community health centers, patients with chronic pain did not have options for non-opioid treatments." There was little to no access or support for alternative therapies like acupuncture, massage, or yoga, which were often too expensive for patients.

"Over my career, I thought one of the best ways to bring evidence-based integrative medicine into the low-income patient population was to use a group setting."

The groups grew, and Dr. Gardiner was able to receive funding for research to determine how Integrative Medical Group Visits (IMGV) could work best and how they could benefit patients.

Dr. Gardiner worked with anthropologist Dr. Lance Laird to marry quantitative and qualitative data. The quantitative portion consisted of detailed questionnaires and outcome measures like pain levels, blood pressure, and labs. The qualitative portion was made up of people's stories and experiences. They utilized randomized controlled trials and clinical trials. They invited patients to sit on an advisory board to gather patient-engaged research, giving them a chance to weigh in on the research methods, measurements, and to shape the curriculum.

Over the course of her career, Dr. Gardiner has had a part in dozens of studies and papers. She's looked at the feasibility of group visits to address smoking cessation in populations with cancer, as well as papers on chronic pain, depression, and how to improve access to group visits.

The graph below shows the number of published papers on group visits over the last twenty years. In 2019, the Journal of Alternative and Complementary Medicine created a special issue dedicated completely to peer-reviewed science on group-delivered services.

Growth in Publications by Year

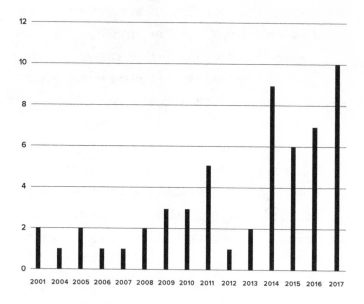

Overall, studies found medical group visits increase patient self-efficacy, allowing them to care for themselves, and increasing self-management skills and self-regulation of emotions. There were reductions in pain and use of medication, as well as the alleviation of anxiety and depression. It lowered costs and effectively offered patients access to care, reducing unnecessary hospitalizations and emergency room visits.

Diving into the studies, we see solutions to problems that arrive in the offices of health practitioners with the patients, but don't have a direct link to medicine.

In one particular study, patients with chronic pain and depression who interacted with the allopathic healthcare system experienced more trauma and pain, partly because of social factors and stressors like racial prejudice, transportation challenges, food insecurity, cultural norms, and housing instability.

Since these social factors were exacerbating chronic disease and depression, Dr. Gardiner and her team were able to work with patient advisors in creating a group that addressed these points.

Using the example of chronic pain, Dr. Gardiner described how individuals struggling with this issue may have lost their job as a result of their condition. They might not have a strong community, or they might feel alienated by what they're going through. If the pain is bad enough, they might not be able to provide basic care for themselves, such as cooking and cleaning. When we're not able to care for ourselves, there's a sense of loss and frustration. Some individuals with chronic pain don't sleep well or don't want to leave the house because they're uncomfortable.

Behavior change is more difficult for those in low-income communities. In these areas, there might not be access to stable, reliable housing, or a grocery store with access to healthy food. Facilities for mental health and wellness might not exist or be financially accessible. In the health-care system, treatment plans might include opioids for pain management, which can be coupled with a stigma or the assumption that they're an addict. The way the current system is set up is so fractured that they might need to see a neurologist for a headache, a surgeon for back pain, or a rheumatologist for knee pain. It's hard to have a schedule that accommodates all those appointments, let alone the transportation necessary to meet them.

A person with chronic pain, Dr. Gardiner says, could lose their job, slip into poverty, go on work disability and receive a nominal sum, lose their community, experience housing instability, food insecurity, and have no idea how to address any of these issues.

HOW COULD GROUP VISITS POSSIBLY TOUCH ON ALL THESE DIFFERENT SOCIAL DETERMINANTS?

In Dr. Gardiner's team-based approach, a clinician and a social worker can help the patient locate resources for stable housing, referrals to food pantries or places for healthy meals, management of prescription medications, and provide social support to help cope with pain, loneliness, and depression. "When we work in groups, we're trying to do mind, body and spirit," she said, weaving together a biopsychosocial solution. They're working on social determinants of health, which includes their symptoms but also their relationships to other people.

The most important outcome to patients was not the curriculum or the physicians; it was the group. It aided in interpersonal growth and learning, increased social integration and altruism, and the impacts rippled outward through the community. People now had valuable support systems to hold them accountable and help show them the way.

Groups Mapped to Biopsychosocial Model

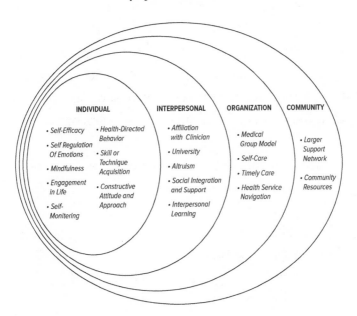

Dr. Gardiner's work is part of a growing body of literature proving group visits possesses the possibility to change the existing paradigm of one-on-one care, which isn't resulting in the outcomes we desperately need. There's a basis of evidence that will allow group visits to be embraced by larger systems. Dr. Gardiner's research shows how "chronic conditions, complicated patients, and preventive medicine, there's an emergent role for group visits." She puts this into practice daily, and works with Dr. Geller on trainings in the Boston area for this empowerment model.

The individuals mentioned in this chapter have created an ecosystem for group visits to really flourish. Thanks to Dr. Noffsinger, Dr. Saxena could adopt the DIGMA framework to her practice and create toolkits for physicians to replicate and scale group visits. Drs. Slavich, Jonas, and Gardiner conducted the research to show us why reestablishing community is effective for health outcomes.

For a movement to emerge and catch fire in medicine, it must possess a few qualities:

- the ability to solve a significant problem that hasn't been solved before
- validation from peer-reviewed literature that proves its efficacy
- resources to replicate and scale it

- a community of people ready to advocate for it inside the health system

Thanks to the pioneers and innovators who paved the way, all the pieces are in place for us to see the large-scale adoption of group visits. The only question that remains is: are you ready?

CHAPTER FOUR

THE CHALLENGES

"Show me someone who has done something worthwhile, and I'll show you someone who has overcome adversity."

—LOU HOLTZ

I've met many people who have tried to run a group and were hindered by obstacles. At the outset, it's really exciting and full of possibility, but an unseen issue can derail the efforts and leave people frustrated. With any paradigm-shifting concept comes the temptation to go back to what's familiar or comfortable—especially when faced with challenges.

You're probably well aware of the amount of work it takes to advocate and implement anything new. Whether it's getting a group of friends together once a week in the midst of busy lives, family, and career priorities, or starting a new method of taking care of patients in your practice, or advocating for change within an organization. The more layers of bureaucracy that are involved, the more chances you'll bump into naysayers who don't see anything wrong with the status quo. Change is not always easy.

A little bit of grit and determination are necessary to overcome inertia and develop confidence in your abilities as a changemaker. In my experience, simple first steps with small wins help build the confidence to tackle bigger objectives. Chapter six takes you through a step-by-step guide to starting and running your first group, but it's worth noting what you might come up against. This way, you're prepared, having learned from those who paved the way.

TENACITY UNDER ADVERSITY

To start, the biggest obstacle to reversing a chronic illness is making the actual behavioral changes. Dr. Terry Wahls confronted this personally, and you'd be hard-pressed to find a doctor who faced a hurdle higher than the one she came up against in her own health. Not only did she overcome immense adversity, she then replicated her own success using groups.

In 2007, Dr. Wahls was in a wheelchair with multiple sclerosis. Her health had been declining for seven years, and she initially took the route of conventional therapy to treat the diagnosis of progressive MS.

It's commonly accepted that MS is incurable. Dr. Wahls read she would likely need to rely on support like a cane or wheelchair for movement, and that people with MS could become unable to work due to severe fatigue.

She started researching other treatment options, but as a physician practicing with the Veterans Administration Health Care in Iowa City, she was very skeptical about supplements and diet. On the recommendation of her physician, she adopted a paleo diet, and added prescriptions into her treatment plan, many of which didn't improve her condition.

When she added supplements, they slowed the speed of her decline, which gave her hope. But by the summer of 2007, she was unable to sit upright in a chair or walk without the use of support, mainly relying on a wheelchair. She realized she was on the verge of being forced to leave her job and accept medical disability.

The turning point came when she discovered the Institute for Functional Medicine. She signed up for a course on neuroprotection. Using what she learned, she added more supplements, started muscular electrostimulation with a physical therapist, returned to a meditation practice, and redesigned her paleo diet, ramping up her vegetable intake to eighteen servings per day.

Within a month, her fatigue reduced and she felt more mental clarity. In three months, she was able to walk with a cane and not rely on a wheelchair. In nine months, she could ride a bicycle for the first time in almost ten years. In twelve months, she completed an eighteen-and-a-half-mile bike ride with her family.

In one year, Dr. Terry Wahls completely reversed her multiple sclerosis, a disease with a prognosis that's commonly seen as incurable.

She didn't think she'd be able to reverse it. Her goal with the treatment plan was to stop further deterioration. Dr. Wahls was surprised by her own progress. It wasn't until she climbed back onto a bicycle for the first time that she realized she wasn't just stopping the decline, she was actually getting better.

The experience completely transformed her understanding of disease and health. With the help of her physician and by acting on this new information, she turned her entire life around. With this first obstacle surmounted, now came the second: incorporating what she'd experienced into her practice at the VA.

As she shifted her focus to diet and lifestyle when treating patients, other physicians started complaining that she wasn't practicing in the same way they were. She met with the chief of staff to ensure she was documenting everything in order to pass peer reviews. Eventually, though, the chief of medicine decided to pull her out of primary care. She wasn't totally surprised; she knew her colleagues were focused on drugs and her emphasis on diet and lifestyle didn't mesh with the way most primary care physicians worked. But what did surprise her was that they actually wanted her to replicate her work in a new clinic.

The Therapeutic Lifestyle Clinic was born: a diet and lifestyle treatment plan that aimed to replicate her results with patients in Iowa. The majority didn't have access to organic food, and the plan didn't include specialty labs. The demand for her services was so high that the Therapeutic Lifestyle Clinic had no choice but to run groups to keep up.

In doing so, Dr. Wahls witnessed how peer-to-peer engagement, including conversation and suggestions from other participants, was more powerful and valuable to them than the physician's input—even if that physician had reversed their own MS. Patients were more engaged overall, and the group lessons were more effective at helping people maintain behavioral changes.

In 2011, Dr. Wahls delivered a TEDx Talk in Iowa City outlining how she used diet to get out of a wheelchair. At the time of writing, "Minding your mitochondria" has over three million views on YouTube. The video went viral and it was so popular that TED added a disclaimer stating that the health advice was "based on a personal narrative." It advised viewer discretion, not wanting to offend the medical community. Hopefully we reach a point where that disclaimer is no longer necessary, because the health outcomes speak for themselves. In 2014, Dr. Wahls published *The Wahls Protocol: How I Beat Progressive MS Using Paleo Principles and Functional Medicine.*

Despite successful outcomes in both her health and career, it was not without significant obstacles. Dr. Wahls experienced resistance from dietitians and medical colleagues. "My colleagues thought I was at best very eccentric and at worst completely unprofessional and dangerous," she wrote on her website.

When a local chapter of the National MS Society invited her to speak, she was interviewed by the clinical advisory committee for the society, who decided she was, "creating false hope in the multiple sclerosis community and was banned as a speaker."

Dr. Wahls didn't particularly care about the detractors

because she had firsthand experience that diet and lifestyle medicine worked. It saved her life.

The National MS Society later recognized the importance of behavioral changes to shift outcomes, and prioritized research and programming that aligned with Dr. Wahls protocol.

She expanded her offerings to host a four-day event that she calls a "group visit on steroids." There, she and her team successfully teach complicated concepts like health timelines, the functional medicine matrix, and functional medicine principles to hundreds of people at a time—effectively proving that the content and methodologies of functional medicine can be delivered at scale, even to populations who previously found it inaccessible. Dr. Wahls notes that this protocol is for everyone, and that it's even possible to follow these dietary guidelines for those who receive food assistance.

Dr. Wahls said, "I am grateful for it all: my illness, my family, my colleagues, the National MS Society, the Institute for Functional Medicine, the Ancestral Health movement, the public with chronic health problems. I needed them all then and now, so I could identify my new purpose: creating an epidemic of health."

Dr. Wahls' story again showcases chronic disease reversal in groups, and furthermore, it shows how tenacity under adversity is necessary. We can all learn a lot from Dr. Terry Wahls, and her story can serve as inspiration as we create changes in health that ripple outward in our own community.

WHAT IF I'VE NEVER ORGANIZED A GROUP BEFORE?

Famed psychiatrist James S. Gordon, MD of the Center for Mind-Body Medicine offers training for physicians in mind-body techniques, which they learn to use on themselves and their patients. Taught in a group setting, they experience the value of this dynamic. Though they make the group aspect very clear in their materials, some physicians are shocked that they're expected to participate in this model. In the second half of the training, they learn how to lead a group, and many discover that they're quite good at it, even if they've never tried before. They realize the setting creates an opportunity for people to learn among themselves and apply what they've learned. The physician is released of the burden of having to focus, keep detailed notes, and address every symptom.

At their first national training two decades ago, an OB-GYN attended who was adamant that he would never run a group. He just wanted the techniques themselves. After the group training portion, he completely changed his mind, recognizing the flexibility and versatility of it.

He's been running groups at his practice ever since, focusing on a variety of issues like endometriosis, breast cancer, and ovarian cancer. He launched groups for women who are newly pregnant, and for those struggling with fertility.

For many practitioners in individualized medicine, they aren't interested in running groups. But the model allows staff, administrators, assistants, and other health providers to step in and lead.

Logan Kwasnicka is a physician assistant at the Cleveland Clinic who had never even heard of either shared medical appointments or functional medicine before learning she would be facilitating the new program. I spoke to her on a tour of the Cleveland Clinic in 2018, where we talked about her experiences managing group dynamics. Earlier I touched on how CCCFM implemented the ten-week Functioning for Life program as a requisite for seeing their physicians, who were overloaded with patients and facing an eighteen-month waitlist. It serves as an excellent example of how institutions and clinics can implement group visits and create a culture of health without depending on their already overwhelmed physicians.

"Learning the material that the patients would need to know was the biggest learning curve, but once we got the material down, it's really just interacting with a group of people, helping them understand their illness and disease state, and it really came naturally," Kwasnicka said.

A team of practitioners and providers lead the ten-week program, but the secret ingredient, according to Kwasnicka, is the group itself. They start out as strangers on day one, and by the end of the sessions they're hugging goodbye, exchanging contact information, and "creating a community to work together toward health as they move forward."

Anyone who has ever led a group knows that this doesn't happen overnight. This level of connection needs to be fostered and nourished.

Kwasnicka found that one of the best ways to plant seeds for connection is by discussing goals. The groups discuss both measurable goals, like weight loss or lab markers, and ones that can't be measured: the ability to run around with their kids again, or go back to work full-time.

When patients are allowed to interact and share, "they bond with each other, and realize they're not alone in their illness. Everyone else in the room has common struggles."

Starting with goals was a sentiment echoed by Dr. Wahls and her MS groups. "If you start with sharing your purpose for being there, it gels the group right away."

WHAT IF PATIENTS ARE RESISTANT TO BEING IN A GROUP?

In the last chapter I shared my own personal experience of being bullied at boarding school for being different. In speaking to people about their experiences in communities, I realized that the environments we're thrust into—family, school, sports, or work—can result in traumatic experiences. It's understandable that most people would be terrified to put themselves in such a vulnerable position, especially if they've experienced rejection or bullying in a similar situation. It can be triggering to share struggles in an unfamiliar setting. Why would we undertake being vulnerable in front of a group of people if there's a chance we might be embarrassed, hurt, rejected, or misunderstood, in much the same way as when we were in school, or in our own family?

The idea of vulnerability is very triggering for a lot of people because we're taught to keep up appearances, have a stiff upper lip, and hold it all together. We're taught to sell the best version of ourselves, and with our newfound ability to do that constantly through social media, it's no surprise we've lost the art of true connection. When we're so focused on "getting" something from other people, whether it's validation or money or likes, we forget that true community is based on gifts and giving.

The groups we're advocating for in this book are formed

around healing and health creation, and markedly different from the ones most of us have experienced. They're not focused on following one leader or dogma; there's no hierarchy. They're facilitated by professionals and oriented toward trust, help, accountability, and problem solving, which creates a very different experience than a high school locker room. In these groups, vulnerability is a strength. Not only are you able to open up, you're also able to get your needs met and receive support from a community. By opening up, you're thereby allowing other people to access this part of themselves, and offer your exquisite attention in turn.

When one of Donna Naumann's patients called for a routine refill on Xanax, she was told the next step was to come in for a group visit to learn strategies to help with stress. "The patient flipped out," Naumann said, and told the staff they couldn't hold her drugs hostage. As a nurse practitioner, Naumann had never seen someone react so strongly to being invited to a group visit.

Eventually the patient agreed, and when she attended the meeting she quickly found herself in tears. She met other people experiencing stress and anxiety, learned about stress management and healthy coping strategies, as well as other factors that could affect her, like diet, hormones, and environmental stressors. She loved the meeting so much she not only apologized to the front desk, she also sent a thank you card and even invited her sister to the next event.

One of the first obstacles in running a group is simply convincing people of the value of the visits themselves. Some people come in assuming the group is inferior to individual appointments. They doubt it'll be helpful or that they'll get anything out of it. Or they've been traumatized by a previous group experience.

Naumann has found that the best way to engage people into a group visit is to tell them that's what the next step is. Similar to how you would prescribe a treatment, she prescribes group visits. In this way, it's imperative to their health outcomes, rather than just an invitation to something they might want to try. She explains to patients that the follow-up visit is a group visit, "and on that day we're going to go over information to help you." The staff then schedules the patient on their way out, thereby automating the process.

The more confident you are in recommending the group, the more confident the patient feels in showing up and getting a great result.

HOW DO WE GET PEOPLE TO OPEN UP?

The key to getting people to open up is strong facilitation. Dr. Alexis Shepperd, a psychologist and life coach, approaches her role with the intention of making a difference in the lives of the participants, fostering connection within the group, and widening their perspective on the world.

As facilitators, we have to "help people get underneath their habitual patterns of relating, which is part of what has caused their health issues, and perhaps their loneliness and isolation."

Dr. Shepperd and other leaders have found that connecting participants to their purpose helps the group support one another in reaching their unique objectives.

It's important to provide clear context of what the group is about to get buy-in from participants, whether it's a group about diabetes or dietary changes. And it's equally important that each participant provides a personal context for why they're present. When people know why they're in the room, and why it's important, that opens the door for vulnerability.

Even though authors like Brene Brown have made vulnerability a more mainstream conversation, it's not typically welcomed or mentioned in the traditional medical system. In one-on-one appointments, there isn't time for practitioners to create a sense of trust that can lead to revealing deeper, more vulnerable truths about the patient's experience with chronic illness.

Within the group, Dr. Shepperd has seen how the extended meetings and support of peers fosters trust and encourages authenticity. She's found that people are more likely to be vulnerable with strangers than they are with a professional. But, she adds, it's imperative that the facilitator also feels safe opening up. Knowing why the facilitator is so invested in the group builds trust. When people are allowed to be vulnerable within a safe group setting, they learn how to do that in their other relationships, thereby bridging gaps to soothe their social isolation.

WHAT IF THINGS GO SIDEWAYS ONCE THE GROUP STARTS?

My friend Dr. Sandra Scheinbaum, co-founder of the Functional Medicine Coaching Academy (FMCA) has a wealth of experience, having led her first group in 1972. Her initial training was in humanistic psychotherapy and she's since worked with many different kinds of groups: women with migraines, blood sugar, breast cancer, adolescence, inpatient psychiatric, doctoral students, and chronic disease, among others. When it comes to challenges on running the actual groups, Dr. Scheinbaum has seen it all.

The dynamics that play out in any social situation can arise in a group setting. We'll tackle ways to get the best out of a group in chapter six when we dive into the details, and it's worth mentioning common obstacles that come up in groups, including:

- Certain people monopolizing the conversation
- Participants who aren't ready to talk, or feel anxious or pressured to share
- People interrupting one another
- Participants giving each other unsolicited or direct advice (which, according to coaching research, isn't effective)
- The formation of sub-groups or cliques
- Comparing success to other people in the group, which is commonly seen in weight loss groups
- Jealousy, envy, or resentment at other people's outcomes or progress
- Diminishing someone else's progress because of lifestyle factors (supportive families, socioeconomic status, etc.)
- Chronic complainers or excuses as to why they can't implement behavioral changes

It's one thing to deal with doubts, cynicism, or difficult personalities in a one-on-one appointment. It's an entirely different animal to address it in groups. Here are some recommendations to deal with common issues:

- A pregroup interview provides an opportunity to screen patients and establish if people have the time, energy, and resources to attend a group (including transportation)
- Reinforce norms and expectations prior to the start
- Having a written form with the agreements and guidelines, especially in regard to confidentiality
- Lead with positivity and act well-intentioned toward one another

Individuals who need more one-on-one care, or who might not be group players, can be given a different treatment plan. Invite a coleader to help facilitate, so you're not alone in managing group dynamics. While the facilitator is speaking, the coleader can pick up on cues that they might be missing and make adjustments. With a coleader, a person who needs one-on-one attention can receive it, which wouldn't be possible if it was just the facilitator in the room.

WHAT ABOUT CONFRONTATION?

For graduate professor and psychologist Dr. Joan Rosenberg, the most important aspect of managing a group is creating a sense of safety for everyone. It's up to the facilitator to bring people back to these agreements during the course of the group. If a facilitator feels awkward about interrupting someone who's taking up too much time, for instance, group members might start to feel unsafe and less likely to share.

Confrontation can be an inevitable part of human interactions. Dr. Rosenberg said, "my whole work is built on my ability to confront somebody and tell the truth to them. What I really believe about confrontation is that it can be the deepest form of empathy."

She gives the example of a patient who isn't making progress because they haven't enacted the behavioral or lifestyle shifts they've been learning in the group. The first step is empathizing with the difficulties they're having.

"I can see you're challenged by it," is a phrase that can be a "connecting point from the standpoint of being empathetic." The next step is saying, "How do we help you move through that obstacle?" By recognizing the feeling or difficulty first, the confrontation that follows comes with a very different tone and intention.

If the concern is that someone will drop out of the series because of negative feedback, Dr. Rosenberg says that can be acknowledged as well: "I want to give you some feedback, yet I'm concerned that if I do your reaction will be to say you're done with this." This actually gives people an opening where they feel validated and encouraged to continue with the group. They create an agreement with the facilitator where they accept feedback and state their intention to stay.

The antithesis of safety is often sarcasm. As Dr. Rosenberg notes, "it delivers a mixed message."

> Essentially there are two types of sarcasm. One is playful and flirtatious, and disguises vulnerability and embarrassment, while the second disguises anger, frustration, sadness, or disappointment. With the first kind, you can be clearer by being more open and direct with your feelings. The second you can be more open, direct and honest about any feelings that leave you angry and upset. The direct approach lets your listener know what you really mean.

The challenges of running a great group aren't just facilitation. Some of the obstacles of operating are outside the leader's control.

WHAT ABOUT BILLING INSURANCE?

Dr. Kara Parker is a physician at Whittier Clinic, part of the Hennepin County Medical Center in Minnesota, one of the few remaining county hospitals in the United States. The clinic has approximately sixty clinicians, plus thirty residents in their teaching program, in addition to faculty, nurse practitioners, and allied health professionals. Dr. Parker is one of two functional medicine-certified physicians, and they have nurse practitioners trained in holistic medicine to support them.

Even though they were able to practice on insurance, they ran into issues with the cost. Since they were associated with a hospital, the clinic billed standard insurance approximately $165 for a thirty-minute doctor's fee, plus an additional $110 facility fee. If a patient has a high deductible, to the tune of thousands of dollars, they could be on the hook for $275 each time they had an appointment. And that doesn't include lab fees.

Dr. Parker and the team realized that group visits could help them optimize their time and make it financially viable for patients. In 2016, she created a four-part series that covered lifestyle, stress, sleep, diet, nutrition, movement, and community. The clinic's residents were able to secure grants to study outcomes.

They're currently only able to work with Medicare and Medicaid patients due to the constraints of operating within the county medical center. Private insurance with high deductibles didn't make it viable for patients. For those on Medicare and Medicaid, she was able to provide "the stuff that standard care doesn't have time for" for populations who have difficulties accessing care. "It's a struggle for them to even get the gas money to come," she says. Wanting to lower the barriers to entry, they started offering bus passes to people who needed it.

Dr. Mikhail Kogan also experienced obstacles practicing integrative medicine at the George Washington Center in DC. Realizing he wasn't able to meet the needs of underserved populations who really needed access to it, he started a nonprofit called Aim Health Institute. He was able to get buy-in, but the challenge was reaching the people who needed it.

Almost immediately, he said, "It became pretty clear to me that the only practical way of delivering integrative medicine to the masses is to somehow do it in a group format."

The first iteration was through George Washington University, which billed insurance. This initially seemed like a great system, but problems arose with payments. Some participants who had high deductibles ended up paying the full amount before insurance kicked in. Other patients had high copays, and since payments weren't collected each visit, they would receive multiple bills simultaneously from the university's billing department. This caused confusion and frustration, with patients thinking there were duplicate charges. Dr. Kogan himself had to call the director of the billing department to explain the group visit model. After a lot of back and forth with no clear resolution, they came up with a new plan.

Dr. Kogan and his team realized they could lower the cost, move to a cash model, and still be financially viable. Visits were about $30 per hour, so $50–60 for a two-hour session. Some patients submitted it to their insurance and were able to receive reimbursements, or at least a tax deduction for their deductible.

"If we see at least eight patients," he said, "we're going to make it sustainable."

In the program, they feed patients at each session. Participants learn how to buy healthy food in ways that are within their budget. They also help with transportation so people can attend class. The program has been so successful they've expanded their locations, realizing that group visits don't need to be run exclusively in a medical space. In researching options, they consider access to parking so participants don't need to spend time finding a space, walking to the facility, or spending money on meters. This cuts down on their commute and costs of attending, which makes it easier for patients to focus on their health, without unnecessary obstacles or barriers.

For anyone who's paying attention, the American medical system is so varied and nuanced that it presents unique billing challenges. Though not insurmountable, they need to be understood before embarking on a new standard of care. Given that things are rapidly changing, we created a webinar to explain best practices for billing and group visits, featuring some of the individuals mentioned in this book. The content will be frequently updated and we welcome questions and input in our private Facebook group, both of which can be found at goevomed.com/billing.

UNFORESEEN OBSTACLES

Though many of the challenges have already been experienced and addressed by the pioneers of group medicine, there are some obstacles that can't be predicted or prevented.

In Houston, Texas, almost fifty people showed up for Dr. Cheng Ruan's first group visit.

The turnout was due in part to his robust social media presence, which initially arose out of a problem: Dr. Ruan felt like the amount of time he spent educating himself on lifestyle medicine was lost time, financially. He combed through data, reviewed scientific publications, and decided to share what he was learning on social media. From there, his Facebook following alone grew to over 600,000 individuals. He was teaching other people exactly what he was learning, and it in turn attracted people to his practice.

Practitioners are always educating themselves, so while the time it took to review all that information initially felt like a waste, it actually helped his bottom line. He had enough of a patient population to attract a lot of people into his new group visits.

One of the main things Dr. Ruan wanted to avoid was overwhelming patients with too much information. Instead of stuffing too much into one session, he focused on what people are enjoying. To make it easy, he and the other five practitioners followed Dr. Saxena's Group Visit Toolkits, using the presentations and notes in the kits (which you can find with other resources at goevomed. com/groups).

Though it can be hard to start up a group, Dr. Mikhail Kogan said, "Once you're in the community and the community gets to know you, the community itself starts to really help you."

As the groups progressed, he received incredible feedback from them on how the practice could improve and continue to meet their needs. This back and forth between patients and practitioners was valuable for all parties, and would prove to be crucial in a crisis.

Hurricane Harvey devastated the community in August of 2017. Though the practice didn't flood, the surrounding neighborhoods did and patients were impacted significantly.

Dr. Ruan posted about it on social media, and both his patients and the integrative health community were incredibly supportive. People sent donations and organized food drives that included healthy foods and items for people on specialized diets. Better Choice Seafood gave them a thousand pounds of salmon.

Thanks to Dr. Ruan's extended network of supporters, they were able to adjust and recover within a month. Many of them met at group visits, and those personal connections were priceless in a time of need. By getting people together in groups, whether in-person or through social media, we're able to create resilient communities. The benefits of group visits extend beyond individual health outcomes and has knock-on effects outside the walls of the clinic.

CHAPTER FIVE

THE
TRANSFORMATION

*"Beautiful are those whose brokenness gives birth to transfor-
mation and wisdom."*

—JOHN MARK GREEN

Early on in his career, Dr. James S. Gordon saw groups as a way to help both patients and staff. His work is grounded in the understanding that "trauma will come to all of us, sooner or later," and "each of us has the capacity to understand and heal ourselves." Instead of treating trauma as a pathology or anomaly, he frames it as an "accepted, inevitable human experience."

The founder and executive director of the Center for Mind-Body Medicine (CMBM) is a Harvard-trained psychiatrist, former researcher at the National Institute of

Mental Health, and Chair of the White House Commission on Complementary and Alternative Medicine Policy. He's also a clinical professor of Psychiatry and Family Medicine at Georgetown Medical School, and the author and editor of ten books. His latest book is *The Transformation: Discovering Wholeness and Healing After Trauma.*

As a medical intern, he became close with the hospital's other interns and they naturally formed a group to talk about what was going on for them personally and professionally. When he was a chief resident in his third year of psychiatric residency, he didn't feel the same sense of resonance at the community meetings in the psychiatric wards. There, the assumption was that "the staff was fundamentally different from the patients, and the community meetings were really to take a look at the patient's behavior, analyze and shape that behavior."

"We're all in this together," he said. "We're spending a lot of hours with each other here in this ward. So these groups should really be for all of us, as a time for all of us to share what's going on, to confront each other if necessary, and to learn from each other." He formed a group of twenty-five patients and fifteen staff who met often.

"That was my first experience bringing together patients and staff to create a true therapeutic community. From that point on, I realized the power of the group. I realized it was crucially important for the patients to have a say, to ask questions about what was happening to them, to question and challenge the staff. And it was important for the staff to also have a place to talk as real people, to deal with their issues."

Dr. Gordon also worked as a researcher at the National Institute of Mental Health, where he organized group visits for foster homes and kids who were living on the street. "I saw the power of the group to give people a place of safety, to be able to teach them things they could all use, a place where people could feel assured of their own dignity, and where they could be active partners in their own care."

Through CMBM, Dr. Gordon and his team work with Marjory Stoneman Douglas High School in Parkland, Florida. In 2018, a gunman opened fire with a semi-automatic rifle and killed seventeen people, wounding seventeen others. It was a devastating incident for the entire community. Dr. Gordon notes that trauma is "profoundly isolating," whether that's depression, anxiety, chronic illness, or psychological trauma. Even if it stems from a traumatic event that impacted multiple people or entire communities, people still feel alone in their experience. Psychological trauma is "a significant contributor to chronic physical, as well as emotional, illness. Social support is the single most important intervention for people who have been traumatized."

After the Parkland school shooting, Dr. Gordon and CMBM worked with peer counselors to create groups for learning mind-body techniques. People said it was the first time they were really able to talk about what was bothering them. They didn't feel comfortable talking to parents or professionals, but in a small group of people who went through a similar experience, they felt at ease.

Dr. Gordon saw similar improvements when he brought a pilot program of mind-body medicine to Kosovo. He and Dr. Susan Lord went to the war-torn country as it was still embroiled in conflict. "It's really important to begin as early as you can in helping people with this approach of self-care and with group support."

There, as the war was just ending, they trained six hundred people in mind-body techniques, including clinicians, nurses, psychologists, social workers, and psychiatrists in the community mental health system. They also opened it up to teachers, community organizers, religious leaders, and facilitators of women's groups.

Over time, they developed a local leadership team of mostly young neuropsychiatrists and a few psychologists. These individuals took charge of supervising trainees and eventually lead the third round of training. In this way, the most committed, gifted, engaged, and respected individuals in the training were empowered to provide ongoing supervision and leadership for the whole program. They empowered community leaders who would then go on to teach those skills to the next round of leaders.

Their work was intended "first, to use the tools and techniques to deal with their own stress and trauma," and then to teach them "how to use what they've learned with other people, individually, with families, in classrooms, and in small groups."

The program is still active in Kosovo, and available all over the country. There, they conducted the first randomized controlled trial of any intervention with war-traumatized children, which no one had ever conducted with psychotherapy or pharmacotherapy. Using the Harvard trauma scale to screen participants, they found that 80 percent of the kids had diagnosable PTSD.

They implemented a weekly two-hour meeting to teach mind-body skills in a group. Psychiatrists or psychologists supervised the sessions, which were led by local and rural high school teachers who had been trained in these techniques.

After eleven weeks of these group sessions, 80 percent of those kids no longer qualified for that diagnosis. Follow-up screenings three months later showed the gains held.

"Rural high school teachers with no training in psychology learned how to use this work at a very high level, and they were able to teach it to other people," Dr. Gordon says. "High school kids learned how to use all these techniques, and their lives profoundly changed."

"The conclusion is that we can train many different kinds of intelligent, committed people to do this work."

After the devastation of Hurricane Maria in Puerto Rico in 2017, Dr. Gordon and CMBM partnered with the Foundation for a Better Puerto Rico to train over seventy people. The destruction of the hurricane was physical and psychological: schools, houses, and businesses were knocked aside or flooded, people were displaced from their homes, and others were without access to electricity or other necessities for extended periods of time. Most of us couldn't imagine the extent of the devastation, nor the impacts of such a traumatic event

When the training began, they were moved by the community's commitment to it.

"We've worked in a lot of different places, but pretty much all our faculty agreed that the people in Puerto Rico are the most committed to learning what we had to teach and sharing it with the population. I think everybody feels so profoundly the pain of the entire island. They're a very closely connected, communal society."

They're now working to bring the training to the entire island, as mental health services were not widely available before the hurricane.

A similar program was implemented in Gaza, where they've since trained 900 people. When Dr. Gordon goes to visit programs, he asks participants what is most important to them, and what techniques they've found effective. One group of female amputees said they loved the group aspect most of all. When told that the group was soon coming to an end, one of the participants turned to Dr. Gordon and said, in Arabic, "You will not end this group." Using a translator, she explained how her son died, her home was destroyed, she lost her legs, and stopped leaving the house. "The group was the first place I went to outside," she said. "I'd stopped shopping. I stopped seeing family. I went to this group. I go to this group faithfully. This group is my bridge to the world, and since starting, I've gone out to see other people as well. So you will not stop this group."

Because of her, they continued the group. Dr. Gordon has seen how important it is to provide ongoing meetings in all contexts and countries, even after people have learned the mind-body techniques. In the United States, for instance, he cites how military veterans experience extreme isolation, as the country doesn't possess the same extended family structures as other societies.

Imagine for a moment the potential of teaching a group of veterans mind-body techniques, which they can then use for their own self-care and wellness, and then empowering them to become peer leaders. These are individuals who possess keen leadership skills and a mastery of teamwork. Veterans listen to other veterans, and there's a level of respect and trust, both of which are huge advantages when reestablishing communities. By connecting veterans, teaching them skills for self-care, and helping them bring that to the next generation of veterans, it is sure to be an incredible force for exponential change.

Dr. James S. Gordon illustrates the power of reestablishing community. His work with the Center for Mind-Body Medicine shows us it's possible, it's viable, it's already happening, the results are phenomenal, it's not limited to the United States, it's not limited to chronic disease, and everyone can play a role.

TRANSFORMING SPECIFIC CONDITIONS

One of the individuals who has radically transformed cardiology by tapping into group medicine is Dr. Dean Ornish, a physician, researcher, professor, and founder of the Preventive Medicine Research Institute in California. As a second year medical student learning how to do heart bypass surgery in 1977, he witnessed patients coming back with clogged arteries because they'd returned home to the same habits that caused the problem in the first place.

Dr. Ornish realized, "We were literally bypassing the problem without also treating the cause."

Realizing the approach to recovery was incomplete, he launched his first pilot study in 1978. Dr. Ornish created a scientifically proven program of lifestyle changes that prevents and reverses chronic illness, with a focus on heart disease.

When patients were placed on blood pressure medication or statins, it was usually indefinitely. But as many as two-thirds of patients prescribed statins weren't taking them after four-to-six months. The limits of high-tech medicine, drugs, and surgery become clearer each day. Randomized trials have shown angioplasty and stents don't actually prolong life, prevent heart attacks, or reduce angina.

Yet the power of lifestyle medicine is evident. "Our bodies have a remarkable capacity to begin healing, and much more quickly than we had once thought possible, if we treat the underlying cause." Patients who were on the heart transplant list no longer needed one after following Dr. Ornish's program.

Dr. Ornish worked with leading authorities in the field, noting, "When you're trying to do something disruptive, it's nice to work with people who have credibility." It's wild to think that lifestyle medicine, or treating the root cause by addressing behaviors like diet and exercise, could be seen as disruptive. His low-fat, low-protein, mostly vegetarian diet is controversial to some. Yet the guidelines of eating real food, less processed food, and more vegetables in conjunction with other lifestyle changes has produced excellent results. Within a cohort, individuals learn the fundamentals of health creation: eating well, exercise, stress reduction, sleep, and access to a community.

In a series of randomized trials, they showed blood flow improved within a few weeks. After a year, they witnessed significant regression of severely clogged coronary arteries, with continued improvement for five years.

It's transformed people's health, it's transformed the system to focus on health care instead of sick care, and it's also transformative for physicians who haven't been happy practicing medicine within a flawed system. "It's been profoundly unsatisfying for both doctors and patients," Dr. Ornish says.

In studies with patients, he asked why they engaged in destructive behaviors like smoking or excessive drinking, and found that they were often coping mechanisms just to get through the day. One said they had twenty friends in a pack of cigarettes, each one always there for him. Taking away cigarettes meant taking away his friends.

"The real epidemic isn't just heart disease, or diabetes, or cancer. It's loneliness, and depression, and isolation."

By getting people in groups, they were able to radically transform health outcomes and treat the root cause: loneliness.

It took him over a decade to prove that this worked, and sixteen years to obtain coverage through commercial insurance, Medicare and Medicaid. The nine-week program is hosted at hospitals and private physician offices in nineteen states at the time of writing. When Medicare agreed to cover it in 2011, their small nonprofit was inundated with requests for training and certification. If a physician refers a patient to their program in the hospital, there isn't an economic incentive, but if the physician themselves offers the program, they receive the revenue from it. It's both economically viable and infinitely more fulfilling than the current model of medicine.

The Ornish protocol set the stage for new ways of delivering care within the system and transformed health outcomes. However, one of the limitations of growth has been the model itself, as the six-practitioner model can be difficult to implement. Plus, in order for insurance to pay, a patient has to be diagnosed with heart disease. All six practitioners go through the training together, and remain together for the longevity of the program. Some clinics just don't have six practitioners or the volume of cardiology patients to make this work.

For group visits to truly reach people, it needs to be simplified, streamlined, and scalable.

Dr. Joel Kahn is a devotee of Dr. Ornish who practices in the Detroit, Michigan, area. One of his patients, Paul Chatlin, decided to organize a free evening get together for other men struggling with heart disease. A few years in, the group has 7,000 members and puts on five events a month, from mini-lectures to small groups, all in geographically diverse locations in and around Detroit. Much of the value of community is recreated at no cost to the participants, no effort for physicians, and no billing of insurance. Freed from the bounds of the medical system, community-led initiatives are exciting in that they have the potential to truly transform even specialized care like cardiology.

In the United Kingdom, Dr. David Unwin and Jen

Unwin, a clinical psychologist, decided to take a different approach to helping patients with Type 2 diabetes. They had very little funding and realized groups could maximize efficiency and allow them to provide support, advice, and encouragement. After six years, many early adopters still attend, which gives hope to newcomers. The National Health Service (NHS) has been supportive of Dr. Unwin's work, winning him the honor of NHS Innovator of the Year in 2016. His practice saves £50k per year of diabetes drugs alone because of this group visit model. The incredible outcomes include over sixty cases of people who suffered with diabetes and are now in drug-free remission.

It's worth noting that because of the single-payer system in the United Kingdom, there are no barriers to entry for Dr. Unwin's patients. While the dietary recommendations and financial structures of Dr. Unwin and Dr. Ornish's work are quite different, the consistent factor is the delivery of services in a group. With Type 2 diabetes and heart disease among the leading causes of death in the United States, there's an urgency to scale access to group care.

In chapter seven, we're going to be looking toward the future, and how other practitioners are transforming other niches of medicine and specific health challenges.

In chapter two we discussed how it is rapidly becoming clear that the era of "medicine for the average" is ending and the new era of personalized medicine is fast approaching—and in a growing number of clinics across the world, it's already a reality.

Many providers wanting to make the switch haven't found a setting or structure in which to deliver personalized care. Others haven't made the switch at all because it seems too inefficient or impossible within the bounds of the system in which they work. For medicine to really become personalized and participatory, we need a methodology that's both efficient and effective. (Any ideas?)

For Dr. Lara Sayler in Wisconsin and Dr. Christopher Mote in Colorado, group visits provided the structure they needed to tackle some of the slowest steps in functional medicine, like specialty lab reviews and extensive intakes.

Dr. Christopher Mote realized early on that "the current medical model has become obsolete and we really need to change it." The backbone of his practice at Cornerstone Health Community is group visits, knowing that "those who need to transform their chronic illness into ideal health need to do so not in isolation but in a tribe." His practice's own transformation started with a free one-hour orientation, required for all new patients. In this meeting, Dr. Mote is able to set expectations for how they practice functional medicine, what they'll expect in terms of costs, and what the group visits are like. At the second visit, the patient receives a detailed treatment plan and a test kit to meet their specific needs.

The lab results are usually the most time-intensive to go through, so patients receive test results at a group health visit: a ninety-minute discussion where people learn about the impacts of the results and receive an individualized treatment plan. Patients are billed for a fifteen-minute office visit, and Dr. Mote said it's been "universally popular among patients."

Dr. Lara Sayler took a similar approach to bring functional medicine to a wider group of her community. Dr. Sayler is one of the many success stories from my first book, who was one of the first doctors to read the book, join our Practice Accelerator, and fall back in love with medicine. Whilst her functional micropractice has turned around the health of many in the community, she wanted to find a way to engage more people into proactive care without having to pay the cash-first visit fee for one-on-one care.

In the rural Midwest, she wanted to offer low-cost options for patients that were easy for them and efficient for her. She created a group intake workshop, where eighteen people—the number of chairs that could fit in her reception—could go through their own timeline and health history, which can be one of the more cumbersome aspects of the functional medicine system. They learned together what antecedents, triggers, and mediators are, how the seven core systems of the body can lose function over time, and how to support function to return.

Participants walk away with a better understanding of their own health, and a personalized food plan. It gives patients a taste of functional medicine, and instead of sitting and listening to a lecture, they're engaged and learning from one another. All for $30.

In Swathi Rao's practice in Indiana, the primary focus of her work is still individualized medicine. She uses group visits as a way to continue their learning after their initial one-on-one care, giving them more information than they could possibly learn in one-on-one visits, and creating a mutually supportive healing community on an ongoing basis.

For the last six years, I've said on the Functional Forum that "the healthiest thing practitioners can do is introduce people who want to be healthy to one another." It's exciting to see the functional medicine community embrace this concept in new and innovative ways. All these stories reinforce that there isn't one perfect system. In the same way we treat complex issues with multiple approaches, we need diverse solutions to create lasting change for everyone.

TRANSFORMING CARE FOR MINORITIES

Throughout the book I've touched on the success of the Cleveland Clinic Center for Functional Medicine and their Functioning for Life program. As chief administrator, Tawny Jones worked with staff to broaden the reach of the program. They asked Dr. Charles Modlin to create a program specifically for minority men. In 2004, Dr. Modlin, a urologist and kidney transplant surgeon, launched the Cleveland Clinic Minority Men's Health Center and the Center for Health Equity. It's the first in the nation, which customized care to the population's needs and interests.

The health statistics for black men are dire, with twice the rate of prostate cancer as white men, and higher rates of hypertension, diabetes, heart disease, kidney disease, and transplants. Additionally, these individuals often don't have the same access to information, education, healthy foods, or reliable healthcare. As Rev. Martin Luther King, Jr. said in the 1960s, "Of all the forms of inequality, injustice in healthcare is the most shocking and inhumane."

They adopted the group visit model of the Functioning

for Life program and developed a six-week program specifically for minority men with hypertension, diabetes, and prostate cancer. It was so successful that participants wanted to continue and it's been rolled out to many of their satellite locations in Cleveland.

The transformative power of group visits lies in its ability to reach individuals who are ignored by, or unable to access, the care and information they need. Dr. Modlin notes that the Minority Men's Health Center has become a "'friendly point of entry' to the Cleveland Clinic's network of care for populations who do not frequently receive medical attention—either due to financial burdens, misconceptions, or general distrust." In turn, the men who go through the program are able to bring that information back to their friends, family, and communities.

TRANSFORMING LIFESTYLE CHANGE

Dr. Elizabeth Markle and her co-founder at Open Source Wellness (OSW) are both psychologists by training, working in integrated primary care behavioral health systems in large healthcare organizations. They both realized "most of our patients were getting the same four behavioral prescriptions."

"Regardless of patient diagnosis, whether a patient has diabetes or depression or hypertension or almost any other chronic condition, and almost regardless of the provider's identity, whether it's a primary care doctor, a behavioral health person, a specialist, or a case manager, most of our patients were getting the same four behavioral prescriptions."

The prescriptions were to exercise more, eat better, reduce stress, and receive social support or meaningful connection in your life.

"And here's the part that makes me depressed," she said. "Providers give these four behavioral prescriptions, some subset of them or all four, and then they say something like, 'Good luck with that. I'll see you in six months.'"

To Markle and her OSW co-founder, this was absurd. Imagine prescribing someone antidepressants and then telling them, "good luck figuring that out." When a physician writes a prescription, it's figured out for them: they send the prescription to a local pharmacy, they make sure insurance will cover it, and the pharmacist is available to answer any questions about the treatment plan. Furthermore, a prescription for antidepressants was a less involved process than a prescription for behavioral changes, which require time, attention, teaching, and ongoing care.

Prescriptions aside, Markle notes that "patients feel

shame that they somehow haven't been able to work two jobs, pick up the kids, shop for healthy produce, prepare it, cook, clean up, help the kids with homework, and then they're supposed to go to the gym and meditate and see their friends." She says "the social structures are not set up to potentiate wellbeing in our communities. Nor is healthcare set up to help our providers be well, or to help them be effective in supporting our patients."

She asked herself, "What would it look like to design both clinical and social systems and structures to make health and wellbeing the default?"

The premise of Open Source Wellness was to design the behavioral equivalent of a pharmacy, a "democratized and experiential delivery system for these basic behaviors that underlie human health and thriving."

"Democratized" is a key word here, as Markle notes that most people don't have the financial and sociocultural capital to access things like whole foods or a private health coach. Likewise, Markle notes that it needs to be "experiential," in that most clinical settings simply offer handouts or "didactic classes and workshops." Markle and the OSW team believe that people don't need more information—what they need is "the experience of eating well in a way that's tasty, and moving their bodies in a way that's fun, rewarding, and doesn't feel like work."

Markle is so keen on the experiential part of it that she even hosts OSW events for the entire clinic staff. This way, all the providers and administrators could see what OSW does, creating buy-in, and increasing the rate of referrals.

Since OSW is experiential, I decided I needed to see it firsthand. On a warm Tuesday evening in June, I drove to Oakland, California, to meet with Dr. Markle.

In the beginning, the four coaches sat together to discuss the session. OSW doesn't hire licensed medical professionals to lead these groups, because the vulnerability and vitality of peer leaders and health coaches has been key to its success. If it's a group medical visit and billed as such, they do have a practitioner in the room, but most groups are led by peers.

The sixteen-week program includes four universal prescriptions: *Move, Nourish, Connect*, and *Be*. In a two-hour session, participants actively participate in all four areas. When I attended, it felt like it was one part improv class, part performance art, part playground game, and part family gathering. The movement portion did not feel like working out, in that we were playing and stretching without it feeling punishing or boring.

For the Be and Nourish portions, we engaged in a mindfulness exercise. Everyone was told to close their eyes and feel an item that was placed in their hands, which we were instructed to feel, hear, and smell, engaging all senses. Eventually, we were asked to eat the item, which turned out to be a raisin, and to do so very slowly. Instead of chewing it quickly and swallowing it, the health coaches guided us to feel how the raisin changed as it dissolved and was eaten.

I remember in school, I learned to eat as fast as possible so I could go outside or leave. It's something I've always struggled with, and the lesson on mindful eating was incredibly eye-opening for me.

We all sat down to a healthy meal, and the participants were grouped with health coaches and peer leaders, with one per every six participants. The meal was prepared by an organization called Food Shift, a catering company that recovers uneaten food before it goes to waste. They provide culinary job training and nourish community members facing food insecurity.

During the session, a licensed provider pulls participants aside for quick check-ins, where they have a chance to measure the progress and health. With the rest of the program run by health coaches, it frees up the providers to focus on care. The group medical visit billing rate is $200–225 per session, and even if they only bill eight patients per week, it generates plenty of revenue to cover the cost of implementation.

The sixteen-week program is so successful that participants are often disappointed when it ends. Some graduates started their own independent offshoot they dubbed OSWx, similar to TEDx.

Markle says, "This just inspires me to no end, because, while clinical healthcare may be the on-ramp for some of these behaviors, for some of these human experiences that underlie wellbeing, really the vision is a culture of health. It's a self-sustaining community that doesn't end when your prescription ends, but is actually life-long and regenerative."

Open Source Wellness not only solved the problem of behavioral prescriptions, they also created a self-sustaining ecosystem, in which participants could become peer leaders. This solves the challenge of facilitating change without overtaxing already overwhelmed physicians and organizations.

Furthermore, with only a sixteen-week journey from disempowered participant to potential peer leader, we now have the right ingredients for an exponential movement.

Dr. Michael O. Smith was the founder of the National Acupuncture Detoxification Association (NADA), which has trained more than 10,000 people—including counselors, social workers, nurses, medical doctors, psychologists, chiropractors, and even outreach workers, drug court judges, corrections officers, among others—in a five-point ear acupuncture protocol.

In Wyoming, the state legislature passed a law allowing US citizens with NADA's training to provide services. This lowered the barrier to entry for individuals to access acupuncture to treat mental and emotional health, post and acute trauma, substance abuse, and chemical dependency.

Recommending the wrong drug to someone could lead to them dying, so it makes total sense for prescribing medication to be the responsibility of a licensed professional. But what is the maximum potential downside risk of doing a meditation or mindfulness exercise slightly wrong?

Approaching zero.

This distinction is what leads me to believe that if we truly want to solve lifestyle-driven chronic illness we need to decouple health creation, or salutogenesis, from the pathogenetic disease care system. The current paradigm was not only not designed to deliver it, the workforce was typically not well-versed in it, and there isn't an existing infrastructure to deliver salutogenesis consistently or efficiently.

There are, ultimately, too many examples of transformation than can fit in one chapter, let alone one book. Major shifts in how we practice medicine and deliver care are happening across the globe, and not a moment too soon. Thanks to all of the pioneers who have paved the way, we've seen the results and we have many easy, adaptable solutions to follow suit—plus the potential for continued innovation.

CHAPTER SIX

YOUR ROADMAP FOR GROUP VISITS

"If you want to empower patients, have more patients than doctors in the room."

—DR. MICHAEL O. SMITH

By now, you've read about individuals and organizations who have already implemented group visits in their community. The intention was not only to show you that it's feasible and viable, but also to give you an idea of the many different kinds of groups that are possible.

Thankfully, there are many resources for starting a group visit, and we're lucky to be able to draw on decades of experience from pioneers who practiced and honed this model. Now, the goal is to make it as easy as possible to both start and continue ongoing group visits. For some practitioners, that means accessing the Group Visit Toolkit, picking one of the niches, and running with it. For others, it means enrolling in the Cleveland Clinic's Functioning for Life training and adopting that model. We'll discuss each of these options at the end of this chapter.

You might even decide to build your own version to fit the unique needs of your community. All of the individuals mentioned in this book were pioneers of this model, and you might be yet another trailblazer the movement needs to thrive and evolve.

One of the most rewarding aspects of running Evolution of Medicine's Practice Accelerator is seeing physicians innovating and learning from one another. Given the speed of technological advances and the malleability of this model, I'm confident we're going to see many more innovators reshaping the structures of group visits. Many of the examples we've touched on so far are in-person, and in chapter seven we're going to look at the enormous potential of combining community and various forms of technology, from telemedicine to online support groups.

Whether you decide to run a group at your clinic, hospital, or launch an online program, this chapter offers an overview of how to start, facilitate, and implement group visits. It's even applicable for peer-led groups.

Whatever your background, we want you to have the resources you need to successfully tap into the power of community to radically transform health outcomes.

What follows provides insight and information into how to get buy-in from administrators at large institutions, a questionnaire to help you clarify what you're offering, a guide to running online or virtual groups, suggestions for maximizing the potential of the collective, and further resources from other institutions and practitioners.

For more resources and updated information, including additional guides to running group visits, you can visit goevomed.com/groups.

TYPES OF GROUP VISITS

The Whittier Way: Lifestyle-Based Group Visits by Dr. Kara Parker and Catherine McLaughlin of Hennepin Healthcare and the Whittier Clinic defines a few types of group visits:

- A standard medical appointment shared with other patients
- An educational approach with a lifestyle curriculum
- Group empowerment with no agenda; the patients decide topics
- A combination of all three

Examples of themes can include:

- **Age-related:** teenage, menopause, healthy aging
- **Cultural:** individuals with similar backgrounds who share a language or culture
- **Affinity:** individuals with particular abilities
- **Chronic disease:** such as chronic pain, diabetes, and more
- **Support:** smoking cessation, reduction of opioid usage
- **Specialist:** functional GI health and IBS, connective tissue diseases like fibromyalgia, lupus, and more

A few pieces of information to think about as you prepare:

- **Confidentiality agreements:** to ensure safety for participants when sharing personal information, and setting expectations. Each person signs and receives a copy as a reminder, along with their commitment to attend each visit.
- **Group guidelines:** behavioral guidelines to help create an open, participatory, inclusive, and engaging learning environment.
- **Individual and group empowerment:** asking questions and for permission, to make sure participants feel comfortable. For instance, asking the group for their feedback on how they'd like to spend their time. Or first asking participants, "May I ask you a question?"

- **Motivational interviewing:** a form of inquiry that asks questions without being attached to an outcome, and supporting participants to make their own discoveries and choices. This helps foster empowerment.
- **SMART goals:** helping participants define goals that are Specific, Measurable, Attainable, Realistic, and Timely
- **Mindfulness/mind-body skills:** introducing ways to manage stress, to self-soothe, and center oneself is a pivotal practice for many participants.

GETTING BUY-IN FROM MANAGEMENT

If you're in a private practice, there are probably very few barriers for you to implement, and lots of room for you to innovate. For those in a medical system or large institution, launching a group visit often means getting buy-in from managers or higher-ups first. For health systems, group visits are not only an efficient and accessible way to offer lifestyle and integrative medicine, they're also profitable to deliver. In large systems, physicians often need to be able to see three or four patients in an hour. It's hard to do that when you're providing comprehensive one-on-one care. But it's easy to see more than four patients in an hour with group visits.

I suggest researching existing programs (like Functioning for Life, CenteringPregnancy, for instance) to see if any of those would easily fit within the structure of your company, as they come with built-in credibility. This way, you're relying on proven, scalable programming and aren't trying to reinvent the wheel. It not only saves you time, but it can also make it easier to get buy-in.

If none of those are a good fit for your work or the institution, the following chapter can give you ideas on how to create your own from scratch. At the end of this chapter, you'll find a list of options and resources. If you work inside a medical system and would like help advocating for group visits, we would love to hear from you. You can reach out to goevomed.com/advocate.

MAPPING OUT YOUR VISION

It may seem like there are a lot of decisions to make, and some feel daunted even starting. Ultimately, creating a new program or paradigm will take some work, but choosing to focus on what's really important to you will make it easier.

It's tempting to want to craft group visits that are for every condition or type of patient, but doing so will only dilute the efficacy of it.

In our Practice Accelerator, each participant creates a Lean Canvas, which is like a one-page business plan where physicians can map out what kind of practice they want to run. The questions, included below, help determine what the problem is, how you're going to solve it, how you're recruiting, how you're going to measure progress, and what the cost structure, budget, and revenue streams look like. The same exercise is beneficial for group visits.

- **Problem.** What problem are you solving? When Dr. Jeffrey Geller started his first group, he wanted to treat loneliness, but he knew no one would sign up for a "loneliness" group, so he focused on Type 2 diabetes. Think: what problem are you seeing a lot of in your practice or community? If you're not sure, start asking colleagues, administrator, staff, or even the patients themselves. You can also look through diagnostic codes in your Electronic Medical Record system.
- **Existing Alternatives.** How are those problems currently being solved? Why is that not effective? If you're not sure, what common complaints do you hear in your practice?
- **Solution.** What's the solution? If the solution includes group visits, how will that address the problem?
- **Unique Value Proposition.** What's the unique value proposition you're providing? What about the group format is effective? What do you, your cofacilitators, your practice, or your community partners bring to

the table? What content are you including in the curriculum and why is it valuable?

- **Key Metrics.** What are the ways you're going to measure outcomes and determine success? What methods have other leaders and innovators used to track metrics? What are your current metrics for success and how can you improve those metrics and outcomes?
- **Advantage.** What are the advantages? What benefit does the group visit deliver that one-on-one visits or other avenues of care can't provide?
- **Channels.** What channels are you going to tap into for marketing, recruitment, etc.? Are you working with existing communities or creating new communities? How do you plan to market it? Are you able to run an event to draw people into the program?
- **Customer Segments.** Who is your target participant? Ideal participant? Demographics? Psychographics? What time of day/week works best for people? How many sessions will it be? Ongoing structures help solve loneliness, while closed groups (with definitive end dates) are best for empowered individuals.
- **Early Adopters.** What are the characteristics of early adopters to this program, the ones who are willing to try something new? How will you recruit them? What are some key words you're going to use to attract an ideal participant? Who is not a great fit for this program and what's the best way to screen participants?

- **Cost Structure.** What's the cost structure? The budget? Will it cost to have a space, materials, etc.? Where am I going to host this? How many individuals can I accommodate? Is this online or in-person?
- **Revenue Streams.** What are your revenue streams? How are you billing or charging for this? Is it possible to use insurance? If this is free, what other revenue streams will help defray the cost? Who is paying? Self-pay, insurance, hosted by a company, sponsored by a brand or city, or is it free? What's the cancellation policy?

A CASE STUDY FOR A PRIVATE PRACTICE

To give you an idea of how to use this Lean Canvas model in launching a group visit, the following is a fictionalized example of a small clinic that wants to introduce group visits as a way to reach more new patients, expand access to functional medicine, and work through the less efficient aspects of care, like the intake forms and lab results. This case study is modeled off of Dr. Lara Sayler's practice in the rural Midwest. Dr. Sayler read *Evolution of Medicine,* joined the Practice Accelerator, and took action on what she learned. She wasn't afraid to innovate and create new models to help her patients, and her practice is thriving.

- **Problem.** It's too time-consuming to go over the extensive timeline and intake form with each patient one-on-one, but it's necessary to get to the root cause of chronic conditions and create a treatment plan. Since it's a cash model, the ninety-minute individual appointment is also really costly for patients, and many in rural Wisconsin can't afford it. No first appointment means no exposure to important concepts.

- **Existing Alternatives.** Expensive one on one visits. Onboarding software. Unsupervised learning from content.
- **Solution.** Start a group visit where patients can participate in their own intake form. In ninety minutes, they'll map out their timeline, antecedents, triggers, and mediators. Lower the cost so that it's accessible for patients and still viable for the clinic.
- **Unique Value Proposition.** Patients can learn alongside peers, asking questions and participating in their health. It is supervised by the doctor, building relationships with future patients. Instead of listening to a lecture, they're engaged and actively learning.
- **Key Metrics.** Number of people exposed to functional medicine per month. Number of class spots filled. Number of upgrades to full appointments.
- **Advantage.** Each patient leaves with a personalized food plan based on their needs, in addition to a completed intake, and health history.
- **Channels.** Email database. Reach out to current clients and ask them to refer friends or family. Contact

people who have been interested in the practice but haven't signed up because it was cost prohibitive.

- **Customer Segments.** The ideal participant has a chronic illness and feels like conventional treatment plans aren't working. They're available for this one-time appointment and know that they'll be expected to participate in the workshop exercises. This person might also feel really alone in what they're going through, and wanting to connect with other people who are trying to take steps toward healthier behaviors.
- **Early Adopters.** Patients with chronic disease who have tried conventional treatment plans and know they need another option. A willingness to try something new, but hesitant to spend a lot on something they're never tried before. Ready to make changes and know they need a structure and support system to help. People who want a quick fix (like a prescription) won't be a good fit for this group.
- **Cost Structure.** Host the meeting in the lobby of the clinic, which fits eighteen. It doesn't cost us extra to rent a room. Offer healthy snacks and tea to participants. Each person leaves with a personalized food plan.
- **Revenue Streams.** Charge $30 for the group visit, which works out to be $540 for a ninety-minute session. Now that patients have an intake and see the value of functional medicine, they're more likely to

sign up for a one-on-one appointment, or another ongoing group.

PRINCIPLES OF A THINKING ENVIRONMENT

Whatever type of group you decide to create, it's important to maximize the thinking of the collective. No one understands this better than Maryse Barak, a corporate training and facilitation consultant who helps create learning environments to foster personal and collective change. She's worked with major organizations across the globe, including Google, Shell, WeWork, and Johnson & Johnson. I was lucky enough to grow up knowing Maryse, and she introduced me to Nancy Kline's book *Time to Think* in 2008. In it, Kline outlines the "Ten Components of a Thinking Environment." My business partner and I hosted a training on these in 2011 and found that the ten components are a great starting point for groups. Here are ten excellent strategies to start you off on the right foot:

ATTENTION: LISTENING WITH RESPECT, INTEREST, AND FASCINATION

Someone once said, loving someone starts with listening to them. Many who experience social isolation are not used to having someone listen intently, let alone a group of people actively listening and trying to understand their experience. This first simple step of putting away your phone and tuning into whomever is speaking is what makes groups so powerful and transformative. (For an example, see the Exquisite Listening exercise in this chapter.)

INCISIVE QUESTIONS: REMOVING ASSUMPTIONS THAT LIMIT IDEAS

In my time as a salesperson, I learned that asking incisive questions helped to shift people's mindset to think of new possibilities. We often limit ourselves with assumptions about the world or our work. An important aspect of a thinking environment like this is motivating people to try new things. If you knew you would be great at it if you did it, what would you try?

EQUALITY: TREATING EACH OTHER AS THINKING PEERS

1. Giving equal turns and attention
2. Keeping agreements and boundaries

These are excellent principles for the entire group to adhere to, and it's up to the facilitator and team to reinforce boundaries. It's natural for groups to have a mix of personalities and characters. Some people who identify as extroverts might feel comfortable talking, while more introverted types could keep quiet. It's important for everyone to know that they have a space when they're ready to speak, even if they choose not to use it.

APPRECIATION: PRACTICING A FIVE-TO-ONE RATIO OF APPRECIATION TO CRITICISM

One reason people don't feel comfortable sharing in groups stems from past experiences in school or other scenarios where they might have been shamed for speaking up. Groups are a space to celebrate the process of learning new behaviors and making positive changes. If we criticize or negate someone's progress, it does the opposite of motivating them. By appreciating people and their efforts, we create a safe space for them to step into.

EASE: OFFERING FREEDOM FROM RUSH OR URGENCY

Most practitioners found that a ninety-minute to two-hour group session is the best length of time to ensure people can interact and learn from one another. Group visits inherently move providers and patients away from the current status quo, where patients get very little time with a provider, and even less time to connect with other people. When creating the agenda for a group visit, make sure you're not cramming too much information in, and leave plenty of time for interaction. It's also important not to rush people to connect, or to show results. Give people time to learn, connect, and heal at their own speed.

ENCOURAGEMENT: MOVING BEYOND COMPETITION

Participants in a group setting are not competing for who loses the most weight or heals the fastest. They're also not competing for who has it the hardest. Instead, they're all collaborators, encouraging one another's growth. This is a great concept to introduce to the group at the outset, so everyone is clear that they're there to provide encouragement and support for their shared and individual goals.

FEELINGS: ALLOWING SUFFICIENT EMOTIONAL RELEASE TO RESTORE THINKING

These components were initially created for corporations, used in boardrooms for companies like Google and Johnson & Johnson, where emotions and feelings aren't often tolerated or encouraged. The same can be said for clinical settings, where a certain level of stoicism reigns. With group visits, we create space for people to share their emotions, processing them in real time. Most people don't have access to a therapist or mental health professional, and some individuals don't have communities where they can discuss their illness or struggles on an emotional level. Creating a space for that in a group visit is incredibly powerful and transformative.

INFORMATION: PROVIDING A FULL AND ACCURATE
PICTURE OF REALITY

What groups have that one-on-one visits don't is the
time to educate patients. There's very little time to do
this in individual appointments, and no way for there to
be space for empowering peers. In groups, participants
learn behavioral and lifestyle changes, receive the support they need to implement them, and interact with one
another in a way that fosters ongoing growth and learning.
The most effective groups are the ones in which patients
have space to speak, interact, and participate.

PLACE: CREATING A PHYSICAL ENVIRONMENT THAT SAYS
BACK TO PEOPLE, "YOU MATTER"

Many people admit to feeling intimidated by or excluded
from the current medical system. With a group visit,
you're creating a space for patients to feel like they truly
belong. A two-hour session allows them to be heard and
contribute. As you start your own, you might realize that
you need physical environments that are conducive to
hosting a lot of people. Most clinics are set up with small
patient rooms for one-on-one visits. Now, you'll need a
space where more people can comfortably gather.

DIVERSITY: ADDING QUALITY BECAUSE OF THE DIFFERENCES BETWEEN US

Another powerful aspect of group visits is how it brings people from different backgrounds together with a common goal: health and healing. Your group might be for one condition like diabetes, and attract participants from other cultural or socioeconomic backgrounds. Or, your group could be about stress management and diet for chronic conditions, which draws individuals who are dealing with a range of illnesses. Diversity is important because we're able to connect, learn, and glimpse other people's lives and experiences.

Sample Exercise: Exquisite Listening

Maryse Barak has an exercise that she likes to run after introductions. Pair up participants so that each person has a partner. One partner is given three minutes to discuss a topic that matters to them, in the context of the group visit. If it's on nutrition, for instance, ask them to discuss what they like to eat or what mealtimes were like in their family growing up.

While the first partner is talking, the second just listens, without speaking or asking questions. Barak says they "keep exquisite attention through their eyes, their face, and they listen to them with genuine interest."

Once the first person has finished speaking, the second person takes their turn to speak. It's not a conversation, and it's a profound exercise because most people are not used to being heard or listened to closely.

In most medical visits, physicians interrupt patients after only eleven seconds of speaking. Eleven seconds! By starting a group visit with this exercise, patients get a radically different experience than their previous doctors' visits. While it can be hard to ensure everyone has a chance to speak in a large group, this exercise is a great way to make sure people are taking turns listening and speaking. This helps all participants understand that the quality of their attention is important. And, according to Barak, "Attention is a learned behavior."

THE PLANNING AND IMPLEMENTATION

Starting and growing a group will be very different depending on your situation, whether you're looking to be part of a healthy community, or in healthcare and advocating for group medicine. For medical professionals, marketing your group visit depends on your practice situation, how long you've been in practice, and how many patients you currently communicate with. We've included some tips throughout the book, and created a specific webinar to discuss how best to introduce group visits to patients and reach potential members. Given that digital communication channels can change so quickly, all of the content will be regularly updated, and we welcome questions in our private Facebook group, where providers can learn from one another. You can find all of this at goevomed.com/groups.

Once you've marketed the program and have people signing up, it's time to prepare for the first meeting.

PRE-EVENT CHECKLIST:

1. Gather materials participants will need for the first session.
2. Determine assessments or documentation tools needed for visits.
3. Decide if you're going to provide refreshments like healthy snacks, tea or beverages, and arrange these.

If working with a team, review the agenda, along with roles and expectations for each person. Instead of scheduling lots of time for lecturing, leave time for group interaction.

At least one week before the appointment, have someone call and remind participants. Let them know logistics like where to park, when to arrive, and what's expected of them. If they have a lot of questions, assure them that it'd be a great question to ask within the group so each participant can benefit from that information. This way, you're not repeating yourself.

Schedule and determine what needs to happen after a session to follow up, and what happens between sessions.

SUPPLIES:

- Name tags and markers
- Forms, clipboards, and pens
- Specialty tools for vitals, patient charts
- Flip chart with markers for notes and demonstrations
- Relevant resources and guides
- Refreshments

DAY-OF-EVENT CHECKLIST:

- Prepare the room in advance in case people arrive early, setting out refreshments or other items to make the room feel comforting and welcoming.
- Ensure one team member is present to welcome participants as they arrive, and help with name tags and any necessary forms or information.

The primary care provider or lead facilitator can welcome all members when everyone has arrived, introducing themselves and team members.

The lead facilitator can model introductions and set expectations for participants to introduce themselves. Pick a format, like stating your name and answering a question:

"My name is ____ and my favorite ____ is ____."

After introductions, provide an overview of the group visits and expectations, including confidentiality. Open up time for interaction and questions. If it's appropriate, try the Exquisite Listening exercise from Maryse Barak, mentioned in this book.

Before taking a break, explain that a team member will take vitals during the break, visiting each person one at a time. Team members are also assessing patients to see if anyone needs a one-on-one appointment.

After a break, open up a question and answer session. Instead of answering each question, open inquiries up to the group: "Has anyone else experienced this problem? What worked for you?" This engages participants and empowers them to come up with their own solutions.

At the end of this, have the group discuss what topics they want to touch on in the next session. Writing these down on a flip chart or board is helpful, so everyone can see them.

Ask people for feedback or thoughts on this first session, and thank them for coming. Now, you can break into individual appointments if people need one-on-one attention. The rest of the group can use the time to interact and connect.

After the group visit, host a debriefing session with the team to discuss what went well and what could be improved.

EXAMPLE OF WHITTIER CLINIC'S GROUP VISIT FLOW

- Welcoming/gathering opening circle and centering practice
- Introductions, checking in, gathering the group's interests, concerns, goals
- Healthy snack
- Movement
- Dialogue on group visit topic
- Mind-body skills
- Handouts and practice materials to take home
- Reflection/sharing the group's wisdom
- Closing circle

After the Session:

- Automated e-mail reminder with information about the next session and a survey, asking participants for feedback and ways to improve

- Debrief with staff
- Charting and billing
- Online Groups

Thanks to technology, we're no longer limited to in-person visits. Using meeting rooms like Zoom can allow providers to include a wider variety of participants. People who might not be able to fit a group visit into their schedule, who don't have transportation, live in rural areas, or may not have access to a practitioner near them, can now participate. It's also a lower overhead for many practitioners.

Most of the planning outlined above applies to online groups as well, but the actual facilitation of it will be much different. Here are some of the best tips we've found for running online groups. This list was crowdsourced from leading doctors in the Practice Accelerator, who had completed a four-part series on creating their own virtual group visit. In chapter seven, we'll look at examples of hybrid and virtual group models.

- To start, **prescreen** participants to make sure they'd be a good candidate for an online group visit. Asking about their motivations for joining the group provides an opening for that conversation. You want to curate a small group to ensure each person gets to share and participate fully.
- Distribute the **group rules** before the meeting, and

post the rules in the chat so everyone can refer back to it throughout the call.

- Create a community where people can connect in **between sessions,** like a private Facebook group.
- At each meeting, make sure each person has their **name clearly visible** on their profile, and turns on their camera so participants are seen. Knowing names and faces helps develop a stronger sense of connection.
- Ask each participant to **check in at the beginning** so each person has a turn to speak and see each person as they talk.
- Start with an exercise to help with **grounding or centering,** either a meditation or breathing exercises.
- Try to avoid cross-talking and **actively listen.**
- If people have questions or comments during the call, they can **add them to the chat** portion so that they're not interrupting each other.
- Schedule time at the end for questions and comments.
- At the end, ask each participant to share **one thing they're taking away** from the visit.

ONGOING RESOURCES

If you're ready to start a group visit and want to draw on existing models, here are five methods for you to tap into current programs or structures. All of these options are conveniently located at goevomed.com/groups.

1. Download a free fifty-page guidebook, created by Dr. Kara Parker of Whittier Clinic and Hennepin Healthcare. In the guide, you'll find examples of various group visits, and checklists of things to think about.

2. Purchase a toolkit from the Lifestyle Matrix Resource Center. Developed by Dr. Shilpa Saxena, the Group Visit Toolkits (GVTs) make it easy to implement and run a shared medical appointment. It includes curricula and tools to maximize clinician time and deliver lifestyle medicine principles to patients, as well as billing guidelines.

3. Connect with Centering Healthcare Institute to see if any of their structures fit into your clinic, hospital, or community.

4. Attend trainings in the Empowerment Model from Dr. Paula Gardiner and Dr. Jeff Geller.

5. Enroll in a training with the Cleveland Clinic Center for Functional Medicine, tour the facility, and learn about their Functioning for Life protocol.

6. Invite trainers from the Cleveland Clinic Center for Functional Medicine to lead a training at your health system, teaching the staff to implement a Functioning for Life program for patients.

CHAPTER SEVEN

OUR COLLECTIVE
FUTURE

"You cannot predict the future, but you can create it."

—PETER DRUCKER

Such are the depths of the predicament that we find our-selves in: chronic disease, escalating costs, physician shortages, care access and affordability, physician burn-out, loneliness, and mental health. Hopefully it's as clear to you as it is to me that group visits not only have a place within the medical system, they can be a foundational infrastructure for the future of healthcare.

In addition to the continued growth of functional med-icine, there are four major trends within this movement that will unfold in the future:

1. The rapid growth of group visits both inside the medical system and outside.
2. Technology-enabled groups and communities.
3. Specialized and specific group programs, whether in-person, online, or hybrid models.
4. Community principles solving problems beyond care delivery.

THE GROWTH OF GROUP MEDICAL VISITS

With the catalyzing support of a storied institution like the Cleveland Clinic, we're seeing the incredible potential of the confluence of functional medicine and community. Though the Cleveland Clinic has been running shared appointments for decades, the Center for Functional Medicine has seen rapid growth in the delivery of shared medical appointments. The backing of this major medical and academic institution showcases how it's not just the groups that matter, it's in pairing them with the operating system of functional medicine that we can truly transform health outcomes.

Over the years, institutions have shuttered because they haven't found a way to deliver integrative or functional medicine in a way that's both affordable for patients and profitable for their practice. Now we have the best of both worlds.

Organizations who have incentives to reduce costs will see the immense value of these methods of care. Where conventional medicine is expensive and dysfunctional, and as payment models move from fee-for-service to fee-for-value, paying to keep people well, the necessity of group visits will be impossible to ignore.

The medical system that's going to solve chronic illness has to understand the causes from a salutogenic and biopsychosocial perspective. Diet, exercise, stress management, and lifestyle habits and the social determinants of health are important, but when people make these changes without the support of a community, it's incredibly difficult to sustain. Even larger medical systems recognize this—Kaiser Permanente launched a new care network to help connect its 12.3 million patients to community services, recognizing that healthcare providers were uniquely positioned to address the social determinants of health. It's the most comprehensive program of its kind. "We built networks for primary care and for specialty care," Kaiser's chief community health officer said, "now we're saying we need a network for social health organizations."

Different medical systems will need varying models, depending on the populations they're working with or the goals of the groups. Dr. Geller's empowerment model holds promise with working in vulnerable communities to solve the social determinants of health in a consistent, ongoing manner. In chapter five we discussed how although it makes sense to deliver these groups inside the medical system—because lonely people end up in the system and there's already a budget assigned for care—the true transformational potential within community is in decoupling it from the medical system.

TECHNOLOGY-ENABLED GROUPS AND COMMUNITIES

As we look to the future, there are many ways in which technology will rapidly increase the efficiency and effectiveness of care, within and without groups. The last chapter included information for running virtual groups with online tools, and we're also seeing hybrid models where in-person visits are paired with a virtual environment that provides ongoing care and support.

At his practice in Houston, Dr. Cheng Ruan is on the cutting edge of combining group visits with remote monitoring, which is now covered by insurance. It allows the clinic to closely monitor the health of patients from home, which also aids in accountability as they make diet and lifestyle changes. He measures things like blood sugar, weight, blood pressure, heart rate, and oxygen saturation, and a health coach monitors the data stream. As technology integrates with our own personal devices, like wearables and smartphone apps, the potential for fully integrated care holds much promise, especially when utilized conscientiously and responsibly. On the one hand, we have patients creating a ton of data, but it remains to be seen how the medical system will utilize it. We are seeing the first signs of integration.

On the telemedicine side, virtual groups can be supported by e-prescribe with Fullscript, where practitioners can prescribe a whole range of nonpharmacological products and services like supplements, to exercise prescriptions, integrated directly into the Electronic Health Record (EHR).

If there's one disease category that is most misunderstood by mainstream medicine, its autoimmune disease. In the pathogenic model, we stray into very expensive autoimmune biologicals like Humira as the first resort, which has no real endpoint or plan to return to health. Whereas with a salutogenic model, there's much more to be done with lifestyle factors, a perfect example of which is the paleo diet and autoimmune protocol (AIP).

Mickey Trescott of Autoimmune Wellness notes that "the process of recovering from or learning how to manage autoimmune disease can be incredibly isolating, especially when a person needs to embark on dietary or lifestyle interventions that go against cultural norms." Food and mealtimes are so much about community, ritual, social interaction, and engagement. Trescott sought out others in her city through an online support group, and they "started gathering to cook for each other and share information about local doctors, food sourcing, and other resources, all of which felt incredibly supportive of sustaining and breathing new life into our healing journeys."

From there, they launched an AIP meetup group on Facebook. It expanded into other cities and now has over fifty groups in the United States and over twenty worldwide, "all focused on facilitating in-person meetups, healing communities, learning, and sharing local resources." Using online tools, they created meaningful offline connections.

AIP can be more expensive than the standard American diet, with high-quality meat and organic vegetables costing more than bread and sugar. By meeting and cooking large batches of food, they split the expense, spend time together, share a meal, and build community.

Sharing a meal is a common way to spend time together, but according to Charles Eisenstein, "joint consumption does nothing to build community, it requires no gifts." By cooking together, sharing the costs and efforts, and supporting one another in making healthy lifestyle choices, we're engaging in "cocreativity," which "is what creates community."

In order to spur continued cocreation, the most important thing we can do is introduce people who want to get healthy to each other.

SPECIALIZED AND SPECIFIC GROUP PROGRAMS

If the way of the past is over-prescribing medication, the way of the future is helping people safely taper off medication and move toward more vibrant health. In chapter two, we showed how expensive prescriptions aren't actually working for most people. In some cases, like with heart disease or blood pressure, it can be fairly simple to wean off them, but one realm of medicine with more difficulties are psychiatric medications.

As psychiatrist Dr. Peter Breggin said, "psychiatric drug withdrawal programs are the most urgently needed intervention in the field of psychiatry today."

In her private practice as a holistic women's health psychiatrist, Dr. Kelly Brogan specializes in weaning patients off psychotropic medications. After healing her own autoimmune condition, she was indignant about everything she wasn't taught in medical school, and frustrated with how ill-positioned doctors are to provide proper informed consent. She put down her prescription pad in 2010 and never looked back.

In my first book I mentioned Dr. Brogan as an example of leaving conventional psychiatry to deliver a root-cause approach. For years, she successfully delivered intensive, one-on-one functional medicine in her practice in New York. As she witnessed her patients transform, she started to wonder how she could broaden her approach to reach more people.

Her first book, *A Mind of Your Own: The Truth About Depression and How Women Can Heal Their Bodies to Reclaim Their Lives*, was written from "a place of righteous rage."

It hit the *New York Times* bestsellers list, and she launched an online program to replicate the protocols of her practice to reach people in the comfort of their own homes. Almost as an afterthought, she created a private Facebook group for members of the course to connect.

Almost straight away, she saw the immense power of connecting those going through the process to each other. In fact, over time, she witnessed how the more she took herself out of the equation and put the power into the hands of the collective, the better the outcomes. "These individuals, in months, literally move beyond their symptoms, have reclamation experiences, and shed medications in what would otherwise, in a one-on-one setting, take years."

People hadn't previously been introduced to other people who were struggling with the same symptoms and attempting to wean off psychotropic medications. The success of her in-person protocol, streamlined and improved over the years, focused on sending the body a signal of safety—on a physical level but also psychological, emotional, and spiritual. What Dr. Brogan realized was that nothing could send the signal of safety more quickly than a community of peers who possessed the same goals.

She followed up her widely read 2016 release with another book in 2019. *Own Your Self: The Surprising Path Beyond Depression, Anxiety, and Fatigue to Reclaiming Your Authenticity, Vitality, and Freedom* shows readers that there are options aside from medicating, and includes a thirty-day protocol to start the healing process. Where her first program prioritized the protocol and sprinkled in a bit of community, her latest program, Vital Mind Project, is focused on community with a splash of healthy behaviors. These behaviors can be simple, like having everyone in the group go to bed at 9:00 p.m. each day for a week, and reporting how they feel to the cohort. The early signs from beta testing showed that it was more effective than her first online program.

Dr. Brogan's unprecedented experience in reversing dependence on psychotropic medications should wake us all up to the undeniable fact that community is an important part of chronic disease reversal. Have we been shortchanging all of our patients in treating them one on one?

As we look into the future, we see the power of the group being an intrinsic part of chronic disease reversal strategies in every niche and silo of medicine, and we have every reason to believe it can work.

In a study from the *Journal of Clinical Oncology* in 2012 found the best predictor of longevity in women with epithelial ovarian cancer were their social connections. They observed participants over seven years, and the 64 percent who were well connected were still alive, compared to the 26 percent of women who were isolated. This showcases the need to implement support systems and groups for those with cancer. One successful example is Healing Strong, which is free at point of delivery and combines empowering information with a supportive group structure. At the time of writing they have over 150 groups in eight countries.

Similarly, the future of medicine needs to find a solution to the opioid epidemic. According to the CDC, an average of 130 Americans die each day from an opioid overdose. From 1999–2017, almost 400,000 people died from an overdose involving opioids. It's clear we need to find a solution to pain management that doesn't include highly addictive and potentially lethal prescriptions.

For those suffering with chronic pain, community is essential in both alleviating pain and the capacity to manage it. Lonely people report higher pain scores. A 2019 study in the *Annals of Behavioral Medicine* confirmed the necessity of group visits to treat chronic pain, as the data showed social isolation played a role in pain perception, coping, and "a comprehensive assessment of the individuals' social context can provide a better understanding of the different trajectories for a person living with pain. [The] study provides evidence that the impact of pain is reduced in individuals who perceive a greater sense of inclusion from and engagement with others."

The authors found that "therapeutic interventions aimed at increasing social connection hold merit in reducing the impact of pain on engagement with activities."

Dr. Robert Kachko witnessed this firsthand when he was in China working on a grant. There, he noticed people visiting a clinic for group acupuncture every single day until their condition improved. Being around other patients gave them a community and a support system of individuals who were going through a similar experience.

In his clinic, patients are placed on an evidence-based protocol, and experience a lot of positive shifts. What they noticed, though, was "a certain subset of those patients would continue coming back, beyond the point that there was something else we were doing on a physical level, or even on a mental or emotional level. They were coming back just to talk."

It made Dr. Kachko and his team realize that with chronic disease, and pain in particular, the role of social isolation needs to be factored into the treatment plan.

Though he was in one of the most populated cities in America, New York City, Dr. Kachko wasn't able to find support groups that were consistent and reliable. He decided to create a system for patients that provided "systematically available social support that can be literally prescribed by a physician."

TribeRx now uses technology to connect individuals suffering from chronic pain. The first half of the twelve-week program teaches mindfulness, acceptance, and commitment therapy, and resilience training. It helps reframe the participant's experience of pain and sets the stage for healing. The second half focuses on lifestyle medicine, drawing in naturopathic principles. It includes "helping people sleep right, to move appropriately for their conditioning, and pace their activity appropriately, to change their diet in a way that won't cause inflammation, and be a support system as they're dealing with pain."

New models are needed to actualize the potential of

functional medicine where there's already good data in one-on-one care. One example is cognitive decline—once considered a natural part of aging, cognitive decline and Alzheimer's is now being shown as not only preventable, but reversible.

Dr. Dale Bredesen is a UCLA researcher and author of the *New York Times* bestselling book *The End of Alzheimer's*. By getting to the root cause, he was able to address the range of factors that causes and accelerates Alzheimer's in patients. They found thirty-six factors that contribute to cognitive decline, and asked patients with mild cognitive impairments or Alzheimer's to make significant behavioral changes. A precision, personalized approach was necessary for results.

This was difficult if they didn't have a support system. Getting patients with cognitive decline to change their behaviors in an outpatient environment is really difficult. Individuals with spouses or caretakers saw better outcomes, showing people need supportive communities. When they're building new skills—like movement, cooking, eating anti-inflammatory foods, meditating—it's helpful to have support. This is fertile ground for innovation and new models for delivery.

Between heart disease, chronic pain, Alzheimer's, dementia, and cancer, a community approach can be transformational for positive outcomes in areas that have been the biggest killers in Western society. This is why it should form the bedrock of an optimized medical system. It has the potential to not only change private practices and health systems, but also entire corporations, cities, states, and nations.

COMMUNITY SOLVING PROBLEMS BEYOND CARE DELIVERY

In the first book, I shared my fascination with organizations that operate essentially as cost-sharing communities. From my training in economics, it's a concept that captivated me because it displays the power of community outside of clinical care.

Over the last few years, I noticed how people's health plans—often colloquially referred to as insurance—played a significant role in blocking people from accessing health creation. With these health plans taking up more and more of the wallet share of Americans, with the average plan for a family of four costing $28,000 per year, there's not a lot left over to budget for healthy spending—like organic food, acupuncture, gym memberships, counseling or therapy for mental well-being.

As a self-employed entrepreneur who is obsessed with resolving chronic disease, this was doubly frustrating.

Even if you strictly follow all of the cutting-edge health and lifestyle guidelines, you, at some point, will become ill. Accidents happen. It's hard to avoid the trap of health-care costs, and record numbers of Americans experience financial ruin from an unexpected illness. People need a way to manage the risk of an accident without buying into a pharmaceutical-first approach to treat every condition.

I started searching for an alternative to health insurance. Ideally, a solution that would be less expensive, more accessible, focused on health creation rather than disease care, and give members options to treatments aside from costly prescriptions or surgeries.

In the 1980s, church groups in America started to realize they were big enough to help all of their members avoid insurance companies altogether. The risk of any one member of the congregation being in an accident or suffering from an unexpected illness could be borne by the community. If Dave gets hit by a car and it costs $10,000, for instance, the 10,000 members of the congregation send Dave $1. This led to the launch of the Christian Healthcare Ministries. For decades, these organizations grew steadily and had several major benefits over commercial insurance.

First, "friends don't let friends pay retail for medicine." As a community of cash-pay patients at the point of delivery, they could save anywhere from 50–90 percent off the rapidly surging prices when compared to insurance.

Second, the incentives were better aligned: as a custodian of the community's pool of resources, members were incentivized to be personally responsible for their own health, and to then be stewards for the health of others and the communal funds. This leads to lower rates of overuse and significantly lower prices.

Third, members could choose any provider, because doctors and health systems prefer cash. As discussed in chapter three, the result of your care is going to be more influenced by the way you perceive that care than the actual care itself, tapping into the placebo or ritual effect. This was particularly intriguing to me in realizing that the majority of salutogenic practitioners were paid in cash.

With these three factors combined, my family and I joined a Christian Healthcare Ministry in 2013 and were satisfied members for years. I wasn't the only one: from 2010–2018 membership of these organizations grew from 160,000 to over one million. The driving force was that being a member of one of these five faith-based organizations offered an exemption to the individual mandate, part of the Affordable Care Act, which forced Americans to buy health insurance or face tax penalties. When Congress reduced the individual mandate to $0 in 2018, we decided to undertake an experiment called Knew Health.

The goal was to see if we could create a cost-sharing community based around salutogenesis, broadening the focus beyond Christian values. Knew Health is the first nondenominational medical cost-sharing organization in the United States. The experiment was a success, leading me to believe that connected communities sharing their costs is going to be an important part of the future of risk mitigation in healthcare—which is currently done by the markets (insurance) or by the government (single payer). Yet again, *the third pillar* emerges as the best possible solution.

I'm not the only person that thinks this. Ravel Health is a startup in Colorado, which provides an alternative to the state insurance exchange, giving its members options built on medical cost sharing, membership-based primary care and wellness services, all for a fraction of the cost of commercial insurance.

With the rise of new technology like blockchain, which allows communities of people to organize without central authority, we are entering a world of new possibilities. I attended my first blockchain conference in 2017, where I envisioned how a medical cost-sharing cooperative, when infused with the radical transparency and trust of the blockchain, would provide a transformative solution to risk mitigation and emerge as the future of insurance. Charles Eisenstein's book *Sacred Economics* uses the example of how Craigslist destroyed a whole industry (classifieds) by not only being better, while also reducing GDP by opening a new channel for goods and services to change hands. We desperately need to access this kind of deflationary force to create a sustainable health system in America.

The combination of salutogenesis, aligned incentives, direct payments, and disintermediation is the future. I'm very excited to support future projects that can make this a reality, especially when it's supporting the billions worldwide who don't have access to health risk mitigation through insurance or government support.

In America, the vast majority of Americans receive health insurance from their company or employer. My friend Tom Blue is a visionary entrepreneur who has helped me understand that the self-funded employer, when it comes to healthcare, is a true cost-sharing community.

"If you define a cost-sharing community as a group of people with a set of shared interests who pool their money to insulate one another from the risk of medical costs (and therefore have a shared interest in the health of the group), then a self-insured employer is definitely a cost-sharing community. Group members withhold money from their paychecks monthly to contribute to a pool, and indirectly, the balance of the cost is funded by foregone income redirected by the employer for this purpose."

Part of the reason why wages have stagnated since the 1970s was that employers were paying escalating health costs. Employees, particularly those with stocks or shares in their company, have all the right incentives to be healthy. And yet few companies have been able to bend the curve when it comes to actually reducing healthcare costs. The 2018 Mercer National Survey of Employer-Sponsored Health Plans found the top three concerns for employers matched closely with the concepts in this book:

1. Monitoring/managing high-cost claimants (who are more often than not on multiple expensive medications)
2. Creating a culture of health
3. Managing the cost of specialty pharmacy

While some wellness vendors have given salutogenesis a bad name by overpromising and underdelivering on actual health creation and cost reduction in an employer setting, we see incredible opportunity for self-funded employers to access the power of functional medicine and group medical visits to control costs and improve outcomes. (More information can be found at goevomed.com/employer.)

Tom Blue's company Empowered Me does this by focusing on getting chronic high-claimants off expensive medications.

"Autoimmune is the ideal starting point for self-insured employers to capitalize on functional medicine because the conventional care pathways lead to indefinite use of dangerous and costly specialty medications. As autoimmunity is known to be affected by root-cause, lifestyle interventions, functional medicine is the only viable alternative pathway for autoimmunity. When targeted to this narrow group of plan members it has an extremely high likelihood of delivering an enormous ROI."

WHAT OTHER ORGANIZATIONS ARE ACTUALLY COST-SHARING COMMUNITIES?

Where the greatest potential for transformation lies is inside sovereign nations where the government makes healthcare decisions. I live in the United States, my mother lives in the United Kingdom, my father lives in South Africa, and I've seen how varying economies in various states of development are all impacted by the rising costs of chronic disease.

In 2017, I had the honor to cocurate a conference in Guernsey, a self-governing island in the English Channel. With the Dandelion Foundation, I helped organize their flagship event: Journey to 100. There, twenty leading health, lifestyle, and longevity experts from across the globe shared insights into how to live healthy, happy lives. The Dandelion Foundation is working to make Guernsey the first nation to get to an average life expectancy of 100. It's currently in the top ten, with Japan taking the number one spot, with an average expectancy of approximately 84 years in 2019.

Gavin St Pier, the elected Deputy in the States of Guernsey and President of the Policy and Resources Committee of Guernsey, spoke at the conference. He stated that Guernsey has the potential to show the world how factors such as community, purpose in life, preventive healthcare, and a proactive approach to wellbeing could make it the first country to have an average life expectancy of 100.

"It is my ambition that Guernsey should be capable of being a test bed for so many different ideas, technologies, and concepts." He equated it to a garden, where they can try things, observe them, and replicate it elsewhere.

The idea is that if we could take Guernsey, a population of 63,026 people in 2016, and transform it into one of the healthiest nations on earth, then we can recreate those outcomes in other communities and nations. How do we do this? By catching chronic disease early, addressing the root causes, and establishing supportive communities to aid in positive lifestyle behaviors. By looking again at Blue Zones, which feature strong communities supporting healthy behaviors, we can recreate the conditions for better, longer lives.

Although the issues faced by people, patients, providers, health clinics, medical systems, and even countries are unique and diverse across the world, the mounting burden of chronic disease is a commonly shared reality. Whereas many solutions being touted are either market-based or government-based, it's clear that Iron Eagle's words ring true: it's time to reenergize the circle. Building on this third pillar and reestablishing community as a structure to transform health is the most economical and effective solution.

For the first time, we possess the proven blueprints to put this into practice, whether inside health systems or in your town. We don't need to wait for the government or the market to solve this problem for us. We can start fixing it today, using online tools to create offline connections, and unleashing the power of community to transform health outcomes together.

THE COMMUNITY CURE

"You never change things by fighting the existing reality. To change something, build a new model that makes the existing model obsolete."

—RICHARD BUCKMINSTER FULLER

While this book has focused largely on group medicine for reestablishing community and solving the vexing problem of chronic disease, this is just one crucial piece on the way to a larger vision toward a more community-integrated healthcare. Over the last fifteen years, I've had the opportunity to participate in and witness different medical systems and modalities through the lens of an economist. In my mind, an optimal medical system is one that maximizes healthspan for everyone and minimizes costs. I doubt anyone would argue on these goals, but there's plenty of dispute regarding how we get there.

In my first book, I proposed that since acute diseases and chronic diseases are so radically different in their etiology and delivery, they need to be treated in totally different ways, possibly necessitating two parallel systems.

For acute issues typically dealt with in emergency rooms and urgent care clinics, a reactive, doctor-driven system built on pathogenesis remains the most appropriate standard of care. The good news is that, in general, we excel at this kind of care. Imagine how much healthier we would be as a society if we were able to take some of the pressure off physicians and systems by moving those whose afflictions are mainly lifestyle-based into a new, parallel system. In a scenario where physicians and staff are not overtaxed or overwhelmed, patients could receive more attention and a higher quality of care.

What would comprise this parallel system for chronic disease? What would salutogenesis actually look like within a medical system? How would it work, and in what order should we deliver services? What in the current system would fit under this umbrella?

If there's one existing model in which to base the future, it's the therapeutic order: a concept first coined by naturopathic doctors Dr. Pamela Snider and Dr. Jared Zeff, which postulates that physicians should start at the least costly, least invasive interventions and work their way up. At the base or the foundation of this model is an assessment of the determinants of health and removing the obstacles to the cure. The very top of the triangle are high-force interventions, such as surgeries, and synthetic symptom relief, or prescription drugs. We should start at the foundation and only rely on the peak of the triangle as solutions when all other steps have been tried to the fullest extent.

High
Force
Interventions

Synthetic
Symptom Relief
Use of drugs to palliate

Natural Symptom Control
Use of natural substances to palliate

Address Physical Alignment
Restore proper structural integrity

Support & Restore Weakened Systems
Aid regeneration of damaged organs

Stimulate the Self-Healing Mechanisms
Recognize the Vis Medicatrix Naturae

Establish the Foundation for Optimal Health
Identify and remove the obstacles to cure; assess the determinants of health

This appeals to me as an economist because we have the best chance of solving any specific issue or preventing the future occurrence of an issue with the fewest inputs. It appeals to me as a human because it minimizes the potential for harm. Given that iatrogenic disease (deaths from drugs and surgery) is the third leading cause of death in the United States, it's an idea whose time has come. In the vast majority of developing countries, there's already an infrastructure for traditional healing, the theme of which is typically salutogenesis and benefits from the full power of the ritual effect. There's been much debate as to how to integrate traditional healing practices and a salutogenic model, delivered in groups, to weave varying modalities which add value but haven't yet found their place in the current framework.

Seeing Snider and Zeff's therapeutic order as foundational concepts, I propose a practical, actualized structure that health systems can easily implement using existing resources.

Group visits are the perfect foundation for delivering care within the therapeutic order. If so much of our outcomes are determined by social isolation, then removing that obstacle by reestablishing community is the obvious place to start. In Dr. Geller's Empowerment Model, we've seen how groups can solve many of the social determinants of health. It's also the least costly and easiest to implement.

The second stage of the therapeutic order is to stimulate

self-healing, which can also be implemented in groups using strategies like acupuncture, mindfulness-based stress reduction, and exercise like stretching, yoga, and qi-gong. All of these modalities become more affordable and are potentiated in a group setting.

The third stage is to support and restore weakened systems, primarily through diet, secondarily through supplementation. Again, this is not only possible in groups, which we've discussed throughout, it's also scalable. Most physicians aren't extensively trained in nutrition, so instead of retraining already overwhelmed doctors, it's easier to deliver education and support in a group format with the help of nutritionists, dieticians, health coaches, and other practitioners who are underutilized in the current system.

When done effectively in a group, using functional medicine and integrated modalities, the first three steps can ensure the majority of populations won't need the following steps, modeling off the success of Blue Zones.

The fourth step is addressing physical alignment, such as with chiropractic, massage, and physical therapy. This is the first step that includes one-on-one care.

The fifth step focuses on natural symptom relief, usually delivered by functional and integrative doctors in the form of supplements.

The sixth includes synthetic symptom relief, where primary care generalists and functional medicine practitioners can choose pharmaceuticals for alleviating and addressing short-term issues with options like pain medication or antidepressants.

Only after all of these steps have been exhausted would we then use high-force interventions in order to suppress pathology, such as surgery, chemotherapy, and autoimmune biologicals.

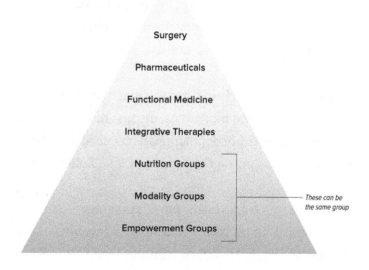

Surgery

Pharmaceuticals

Functional Medicine

Integrative Therapies

Nutrition Groups

Modality Groups — These can be the same group

Empowerment Groups

The only thing I dislike about the therapeutic order is that it's constructed as a pyramid. Ultimately, we are moving away from the era of the pyramid and toward the circle.

We've seen this in other areas, where the pyramid has been traded in for forms that closely match our day-to-day experience. You might remember how the United States Department of Agriculture once utilized a food pyramid to illustrate dietary guidelines. In 2011, the USDA switched the pyramid to a circle so it resembles a plate. Though it's still not optimal, it's an improvement in the sense that it more closely aligns to how people make daily food choices.

Similarly, the therapeutic order would benefit from moving away from the triangle or pyramid, which connotes a certain hierarchy. Within the triangle, the medical system holds the power at the peak, providing life-saving surgeries or access to pharmaceuticals. At the bottom are the aspects of health creation that are left to the patient, including the social determinants of health. This structure feels similar to that of the hospital system itself, which is hierarchical in nature, rooted in the old paradigms and a disease-centric approach.

If we're going to reestablish community, the more appropriate metaphor or model is a circle. My unified thesis "The Community Cure" is built on 5 C's, and in this structure, the cost of care delivery increases as you move toward the center. Like the therapeutic order, the goal is to keep people healthy and out of the medical system with the minimum possible inputs.

1. **Culture:** The outer layer of the circle is creating a culture of health. In chapter seven we saw how this is a priority for self-funded employers, but in reality, this should be a priority everywhere—whether we're in a private practice, major health systems, small towns, big cities, or nationwide. It's easy to build a culture of health in small groups and intimate environments. This can be delivered through educational content, which is nearly free at point of delivery, decentralized, broadcast and disseminated through every available channel.

2. **Community:** The next layer is community, where people have access to a supportive network of individuals to aid them in activating the culture of health. People are able to both learn new habits and reinforce positive behaviors. Groups are an obvious delivery system for establishing community, and economically viable for everyone.

3. **Coaching:** With coaching, individuals can work with trained professionals like health coaches to reach their goals, whether they're reversing chronic disease, or working toward developing balanced lifestyle choices. This is either an affordable layer of one-on-one care that can help overcome individual blockages at a fraction of the cost of healthcare, or facilitated in groups.

4. **Care:** For those who have gone through all of these options without resolution, the next step is care. Similar to steps five and six of the pyramid, this can

address acute issues and accidents as they arise, as well as chronic ones that have been resistant to resolution through less expensive inputs. The aim is still salutogenesis, weaning people off medication and getting them back to a foundation of good health. This is where we enter the world of licensed medical professionals and can include primary care, functional medicine, specialty care, chiropractic, and physical therapy.

5. **Cost Sharing:** At the center is cost sharing. For all of the areas of health where we need care—surgery, accidents, transplants, serious chronic illness, cancer—there should be readily available funds to ensure everyone can access a high-quality treatment plan and trained professionals. It's inevitable that we'll all fall ill at some point, even despite our best efforts. Essentially the community takes care of unexpected illnesses, afflictions, care delivered by specialists, drugs, emergency rooms, urgent care, and more.

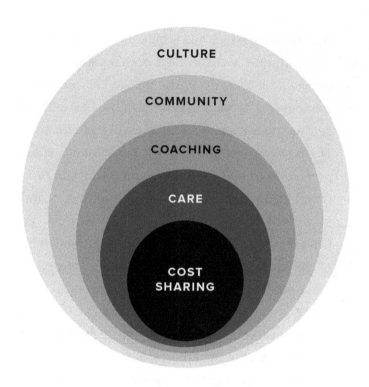

CULTURE

COMMUNITY

COACHING

CARE

COST
SHARING

Building up culture and community will help people stay out of the disease care system, and maintain a higher level of health and standard of living than we're currently experiencing.

Different organizations can deliver different parts of the 5 C's. A fully integrated system in a major institution or a self-funded employer could provide all five, whereas a local heart disease support group can tap into Culture, Community, and possibly Coaching. A functional medicine practitioner could deliver the first four C's, and partner with a hospital for the Cost-Sharing portion. In my personal experience, I connect with Culture, Community, and Coaching through my local Crossfit box, and attend a weekly men's group. I see a functional medicine doctor for Care, and my family and I are healthy enough to not rely on their services often. For the Cost-Sharing portion, I'm a member of a cost-sharing community. Though I have yet to make a claim in seven years, there's peace of mind knowing that if an unexpected cost arises, I can depend on the support of the community to share the costs. It took me fifteen years to find the perfect framework for maximizing health at minimum costs, not just for myself but for others, and I intend to spend the next fifty years advocating for this future.

The Community Cure is about reestablishing community, plain and simple. If the most important determinant of health is loneliness and social isolation, we need to get to the root cause.

Delivering groups inside the healthcare system is the first step. It makes sense to initiate this here because it's where lonely people end up, and where the infrastructure and budget currently exists for the necessary work of alleviating social isolation. The medical system itself is overwhelmed, crumbling under the current system of care, so by introducing people who want to get healthy to each other, everyone thrives. This is a scenario and a future in which all parties who matter win: patients, practitioners, providers, and health systems.

The most exciting part of healing in groups is not only the transformative experiences of participants, but how quickly they turn around and become the next generation of teachers, leading family, friends, and even colleagues to bettering their health. The era of the individual expert is being replaced by the era of the collective.

Sometimes the problems we see in healthcare seem insurmountable. The solution to insurmountable problems is exponential solutions.

FURTHER RESOURCES

For the full episodes, interviews, and presentations mentioned in this book, visit goevomed.com/thecommunitycure

CHAPTER ONE

Evolution of Medicine Podcast Group Visit Series, Part 1: Lessons from Two Decades of Group Visits, featuring Dr. Jeffrey Geller

September 2019 Functional Forum: Integrative Medicine for the Underserved

CHAPTER TWO

Evolution of Medicine Podcast Group Visit Series, Part 3: The Cleveland Clinic is "Functioning for Life," featuring Tawny Jones

Big Bold Health Podcast

Next Steps For Group Training: CCCFM's Functioning for Life™

CHAPTER THREE

Evolution of Medicine Podcast Group Visit Series, Part 4: Making it Easy to Replicate, featuring Shilpa P. Saxena, MD

Next Steps for Group Training: Lifestyle Matrix Resource Center Group Visit Toolkit

CHAPTER FOUR

Evolution of Medicine Practice Accelerator: Scaling the Wahls Protocol with Groups, featuring Dr. Terry Wahls

Evolution of Medicine Podcast: Evolution of Primary Care—Group Visits, featuring Kara Parker, MD

Evolution of Medicine Podcast Group Visit Series, Part 2: Mental Health and Medicaid, featuring Mikhail Kogan, MD

CHAPTER FIVE

Functional Forum: Can You Practice Integrative Medicine on Insurance? An Interview With Dean Ornish

Evolution of Medicine Podcast Group Visit Series, Part 6: Lab Review in a Group, featuring Christopher Mote, DO, DC, IFMCP

Evolution of Medicine Podcast Group Visit Series, Part 7: YOUniversity, featuring Lara Salyer, DO, IFMCP

CHAPTER SIX

"The Whittier Way: Lifestyle-Based Group Visits" guide by Dr. Kara Parker and Catherine McLaughlin of Hennepin Healthcare and the Whittier Clinic

Evolution of Medicine Practice Accelerator

CHAPTER SEVEN

October 2019 Function Forum: Chronic Pain—A Biopsychosocial Approach

Evolution of Medicine Podcast: Can You Create a Blue Zone? The 64,000 Person Question

Journey to 100, coorganized by *Evolution of Medicine* and the Dandelion Foundation

The Daniel Plan: 40 Days to a Healthier Life by Daniel Amen, MD, Mark Hyman, MD, and Rick Warren

A Mind of Your Own: The Truth About Depression and How Women Can Heal Their Bodies to Reclaim Their Lives by Kelly Brogan, MD

Own Your Self: The Surprising Path Beyond Depression, Anxiety, and Fatigue to Reclaiming Your Authenticity, Vitality, and Freedom by Kelly Brogan, MD

Sacred Economics: Money, Gift, and Society in the Age of Transition by Charles Eisenstein

The Transformation: Discovering Wholeness and Healing After Trauma by James S. Gordon, MD

How Healing Works: Get Well and Stay Well Using Your Hidden Power to Heal by Dr. Wayne Jonas

The Third Pillar: How Markets and the State Leave the Community Behind by Raghuram Rajan

ACKNOWLEDGMENTS

Writing this book has been deeply personal for me, it is so important to share the thanks to all those who made it possible.

First and foremost, a big thank you to my wife Rachel who has been supporting "The James show" for more than fourteen years. We lived together in community when we first met, and most of my conviction that this is a worthy way to spend our lives comes from thousands of conversations, musings, and pillow talk of two people drawn together to do this work. I love you. I love our family and I appreciate everything you bring to our team.

Thanks to my daughter, Kaliana, who forced us to understand the critical nature of authentic community and rhythm. To see you blossom is such a gift.

Thanks to my parents for setting such a great example of courageous and aligned living, dedicated to the pursuit of universal truth.

I want to sincerely thank all the people that appear in this book, who gave their time freely so I could learn from them and turn their stories into a narrative that, hopefully, moves the needle. I hope this book can be the "hundredth monkey" of the group visit movement, transmitting it further into the collective consciousness.

And to all those people who have been doing their work on the front lines of healthcare without recognition, thank you. The patterns of cause and effect are almost impossible to comprehend in a world so complex and interconnected, and it is clear to me that nothing generates a more powerful ripple that empowering people into understanding themselves and their health.

Special thanks to John Weeks who introduced me to a number of the people featured in this book and has been encouraging me to follow this path for years. Thanks to Marc Winn, JJ Virgin, and Erik Goldman for giving me a chance to share my truth on your stages.

To Charles Eisenstein and Dr. Kelly Brogan whose writing always inspires me, and have lit the path toward the story of interbeing.

Thanks to Dr. Mark Hyman who has been beating the community drum for a decade and has been generous with his time and support, and Dr. Jeffrey Bland for his constant encouragement and, in the last two years, specific mentorship that has changed the way I think about what I am capable of for the better.

Thanks to the members of the Evolution of Medicine *Practice Accelerator* who came together to coimagine what the *virtual group visit* could be and shared valuable wisdom for this book.

Thanks to the team at the Lifestyle Matrix Resource Center who supported the podcast series this year, and have been a big reason why this book came together so effortlessly.

Thanks to my editor Elizabeth de Cleyre, editing the manuscript with you in real time over a Zoom call is one of my favorite past times, and it likely won't be the last.

Finally, thanks to my business partner Gabriel Victor Hoffman, who passed away on April 22 of this year. For ten years we discussed healthcare transformation through community and coaching, and this is a tribute to you. Thank you Alee for channeling his wisdom for this book in his physical absence.

And thanks to you, the reader, for taking the time to absorb these concepts. The virus is planted, let's hope it goes systemic.

ABOUT THE AUTHOR

With the soul of an advocate and the mind of an entrepreneur, **JAMES MASKELL** has spent the past decade
innovating at the cross section of functional medicine
and community. To that end, he created the Functional
Forum, the world's largest integrative medicine conference with record-setting participation online and
growing physician communities around the world. His
organization and bestselling book of the same name,
Evolution of Medicine, prepares health professionals for
this new era of predictive, preventive medicine. He is an
in-demand speaker and impresario, being featured on
TEDMED, HuffPost Live, and TEDx, as well as lecturing internationally.